Jim Craig's BATTLE FOR BLACK ROCK

by

Ralph Connor

Edited by Michael Phillips
for the Sunrise *Stories of Yesteryear* series

SUNRISE BOOKS
PUBLISHERS

EUREKA, CALIFORNIA 95501
A Division of One Way, Ltd.

Originally published as *Black Rock*. Privately printed in Canada by Jim MacDonald in 1898 and then in the United States in 1900 by Fleming H. Revell.

This edited edition, *Jim Craig's Battle for Black Rock*, Copyright © 1988 by Sunrise Books, Published as Volume 1 in the Sunrise "Stories of Yesteryear" Series.

Printed in the United States of America

Library of Congress Catalog Card Number
88-60833

ISBN 0-940652-06-4

DEDICATION

To Kent Bateman,
whose love for Ralph Connor played
a significant role in the inauguration
of this new series, and a man whose
priorities, ministry, and compassion
for his fellow man in many ways mirror
Connor's own.

THE SUNRISE STORIES
OF YESTERYEAR

Stories of Yesteryear is a series of novels which hearkens back to nostalgic times of bygone years —times which, if not easier, somehow yet seem less complex, even with their hardships, than these present frenzied years of the late 20th century. The series includes old publications which have been lost to the present day reading public, but which in their own day were best-sellers. Most of these have been edited for Sunrise and brought back into print in updated format so that you can today enjoy quality, wholesome fiction through great works and classics of the past. In addition the series will occasionally offer new stories about historical times and places of past generations. All the books in the *Stories of Yesteryear* series are stories about people with real joys and problems you can identify with. They are uplifting and inspirational in their content, while not always heavily "spiritual." They will be enjoyable and dramatic stories, books you can be proud to read and give to friends. We at Sunrise Books hope you will enjoy the selections chosen for this series. We are always happy for your comments about any of our books.

CONTENTS

INTRODUCTION

I have a love, sometimes even a passion, for old things.

Old tables, old barns, old landscapes, old mountains, old castles, old gardens, old bureaus, old buildings, and old books. I especially love history—old *times*.

Out of this has emerged from within me a hunger to write and edit and publish books which hearken back to nostalgic bygone years—times which, if not easier, somehow seem less complex, even with their hardships, than these present frenzied years of the 20th century. It is not that "old" is necessarily better by some absolute standard. Yet the flood of "newness" which contemporary society presses upon us tends to drown out the sometimes quieter voices from the past. And it is my conviction that these ancient voices, though perhaps expressing themselves in different, occasionally in quaint and old-fashioned ways, nevertheless contain much truth for us today.

Thus, coupled with my interest in reading and writing historical fiction is an ever-present itch to uncover and bring to light old books which have for one reason or another been lost to the reading public. It has grown almost to a compulsion to discover the works of forgotten authors, and then do what I can to bring their works back into print. Sometimes this will mean simply reprinting them. Other times it may mean a thorough editing of every line or a change in format. But always the goal is that present day readers of quality, wholesome, inspiring fiction can once again enjoy works and classics of the past.

It was this desire which led to the edited editions of George MacDonald's classics which I have done for Bethany House Publishers. And now I am excited to be able to introduce you—through this series for Sunrise Books—to another nearly-forgotten author of three generations past, whose life and whose books in certain ways parallel MacDonald's own.

I first heard of Ralph Connor (1860-1937) several years ago through two friends who kept telling me, "You really ought to read some of Ralph Connor's books. They're terrific!"

But I was busy, and never got around to doing so.

Yet these men were persistent. And I found their urgings especially difficult to ignore in that they came from such different quarters and had such different reading tastes. Both were close friends of mine. One man pastored a small church, did carpentry work on the side, and enjoyed reading, in addition to Connor, the likes of Harold Bell Wright and similar fiction. The other was a seminary Professor with many literary accolades to his credit, whose chief reading interest was not in the line of fiction at all but in weighty theological treatises.

I respected and admired both men, diverse as they were, and each kept saying, "You've got to read Connor." And it was my seminary Ph.D. friend who said, "You have no idea how that man influenced me when I was young. I read his books, and they instilled within me such a sense of goodness and strong, manly uprightness. The men, the heroes of his books have remained with me all my life, and have been very influential in the person I am today. Here," he went on—and I can picture the moment even now with a sigh of mingled sadness and rejoicing, for the man has since gone home to be with his Lord—"here...take this copy of mine and see what you think."

Thus, eventually I began to thumb my way through these old worn copies of Connor's books, some of them more than 80 years old, at first out of loyalty to my two friends. Pretty soon I started to hunt for them myself, a curiosity beginning to rise within me to find out the answer to the question: "Just who *is* Ralph Connor anyway?"

As I began to investigate this Canadian writer of the early 20th century, my interest could not help but be aroused. I discovered that, though a pastor of a Winnipeg church for most of his professional life, almost incidentally he stumbled into writing on the side. In so doing he gained a worldwide reputation for a name which was not even his own, eventually penning some twenty-five novels, many of which were best-sellers in the early years of this century. His first five titles alone sold some two million combined copies within their first several years, and the total volume of his work was estimated to be over five million. But as popular as he had once been, upon further investigation I discovered that only three or four of his works were still in print, and these were being sold only in very expensive library editions. There was not a single book of this once best-selling author still readily available to the book-buying public.

Charles William Gordon was born in Glengarry, Ontario, the son of a Scottish Highland Presbyterian minister. His mother was also of Scottish descent, and his Scottish roots— vividly visible in everything about him, down to his very name and place of birth—always played an intrinsic role in the stories and characters of the later author's writings.

Scotland's "Highland Clearances" of the late 18th and early 19th centuries had resulted in a steady influx of Scottish immigrants to Canada (as recounted in the MacDonald title *The Highlander's Last Song*).

Gordon's parents had emigrated from Scotland not long

before their son's birth, still spoke the "auld Scot's tongue" at home, and thus the Scottish Highland past of the Gordon family never left them. Even the hometown name of Glengarry, hearkens back to "the old country," as do many place names in Canada, indicating the reestablishment of little Scottish communities throughout the new land. And the wild scenery of the region lingered long in young Charles Gordon's memory. His later books are liberally sprinkled with Scottish characters, Scottish songs, and even Scottish dialect.

Gordon worked his way through the University of Toronto with his brother, taught for a year, and then put himself through the divinity school, Knox College. The two years 1883-1885 followed at the University of Edinburgh in Scotland, after which Gordon returned to Canada, where he became a young missionary to the miners, lumbermen, and ranchers of the Canadian Rocky Mountains.

It was during his years in western Canada, living with the rough and tumble men of the mountains and prairies, that Gordon's writing career really began, though he did not suspect it at the time. His sensitive spirit fell in love with these men, while at the same time recoiled from the godlessness of their lifestyles and the bondage to alcohol under which many of them lived. He loved the West and never forgot it. Neither did he forget the men he had met, shared life with, and come to love.

But most of all he never forgot the vision which burned in his heart to tell them of God's love. He yearned to help them make something better of themselves.

He spent only a few years in the West. But coming as they did in the formative years of his late 20's, the images and faces and dreams and hopes of that period became a foundation for much of his later life.

Gordon was a missionary, an evangelist, at heart—a man whose soul burned with a passion for the eternal salvation of men. He traveled to the West as a young and untried missionary, walked alone into regions where no churches existed, where the men drank hard, carried guns, settled disputes with their fists, and were uninterested in the gospel. Into such a setting he went, as a greenhorn, so to speak, carrying a Bible instead of a six-shooter, and speaking words of peace and gentleness and compassion. The impact of his life in the West is left to the reader of his books to determine.

In 1894, after some years in the West, Gordon became the minister of St. Stephen's Church in Winnipeg. Winnipeg was then a booming town on the edge of Canada's Western frontier, a thorough mix of East and West, where a real estate developer from Chicago or Montreal, a fur-trapper down from the mountain country, and a gun-toting cattleman from the plains might share a table together at the local boarding house. Into this milieu came 34-year old Charles Gordon to attempt to extend his evangelistic vision into the city. His "church" at St. Stephens was in reality but a tiny mission outreach—an inauspicious beginning for the young preacher.

But Winnipeg was a thriving young place, full of enthusiasm for the future. And Gordon's impact and missionary zeal was quickly felt. As he himself later recalled: "The story of St. Stephen's Church is quite a remarkable one. It was my good fortune to be its first minister. The growth of the church was extraordinary. One secret was youth. The city was young, the people young, the minister young. At my first communion in 1894 the roll showed fourteen members."

Youth notwithstanding, Gordon modestly omits mention of his own key role in the growth and outreach of the ministry of St. Stephens. He remained minister there for 40 years, and by 1914 there were over 1,000 members on the same roll and the church had found it necessary to enlarge seven times, so active were its people in many aspects of ministry.

Gordon served as chaplain of the 43rd Cameron High-landers division in World War I, and through his increasing reputation (both as a writer and as a minister) he was later involved in national positions, campaigning for the League of Nations, serving as chairman of the Manitoba Council of Industry and as Moderator of the General Presbyterian Assembly in Canada.

He married Helen King, daughter of a fellow clergy-man, in 1898 and their marriage was a long and happy one, with seven children—the eldest a son, the other six daughters. His college days, as well as his missionary experiences in the Rockies, always remained fond in his memory. He was an athlete, a singer, a champion canoeist, all disciplines which stemmed from his days at the University, and mention of which repeatedly found their way into his books. He loved the out of doors and his "summer home" was really nothing but a camp in the woods.

Gordon became an author by accident.

In 1897 Gordon was sent to Toronto to meet the Presbyterian General Assembly as a representative of the Western Home Mission Committee in hopes of inspiring his church's leaders about this aspect of ministry. He was shocked by the seeming indifference of the Assembly toward the mission work being carried out in the small new mining centers in the mountains, and by its lack of concern for the pastors with their small congregations in the foothill country. As excited as he still was about such endeavors himself, it grieved him to see such a lackadaisical attitude on the part of the Church leaders. Something had to be done, he felt, to awaken them, and all of Canada.

After the meeting Gordon went to see his old friend, Rev. Jim MacDonald, who was then the editor of the church paper, the *Westminster Magazine*.

In MacDonald's office he let himself go, decrying the apathy of the Assembly, and giving his friend a full portrait of a trip he had recently taken to visit many of the missionary outposts of the west. Of the private meeting, he later remarked, "My language, I will confess, would have required editing before publication."

"Sit down, Gordon," urged MacDonald. "Be calm!"

It was the wrong word to use on the young firebrand preacher. And for the next fifteen minutes MacDonald sat listening to more of Gordon's tales.

"Well, what are you going to do about it?" MacDonald asked when he was through.

"What are *you* going to do about it?" Gordon shouted back at him. "What's that sanctimonious *Westminster* of yours going to do about it?"

More heated debate followed. Then suddenly MacDonald had an idea.

"But say, Charles, my boy," he said eagerly, "—I've got it! I've got it! You write me something when you go back to Winnipeg!"

"Me write? What good would that do?"

"Tell the people what's going on out there. Oh, not like some committee report, but a little personal thing. A story out of your own experience—put it in the form of a yarn! Yes, that's it!"

MacDonald's hands raked through his shock of red hair. He sprang to his feet and began pacing the room.

"Charles! I have got it! A story! You remember that thing you did years ago about your first summer in Southern Manitoba. That's it! Promise me you'll do it!"

"I'll think about it."

"Think about it? I know you too well. No! Before you leave this room you will give me your word of honor that you will write me a short sketch. I'll put it in my Christmas issue of the magazine."

Gordon's own words describe the result of that conversation:

"I promised and left him...When I reached Winnipeg I was so overwhelmed with back work that any attempt to write my sketch was impossible. Soon I began to get letters from the editor of the *Westminster*—then telegrams—I cursed him in my heart. But one Wednesday night after coming home from my prayer meeting I sat down, took pencil and notebook and at three o'clock Thursday morning I had in my hand: *Christmas Eve in a Lumber Camp*.

"With scarcely a word of retouching I sent it to Jim MacDonald.

"In a few days a wire came: 'Ms. too long for single article. Re-write. Make it into three.'

"I was too late for the Christmas number. I went at the thing with more care and deliberation, and in ten days I had a story in three chapters. That story was the beginning of *Black Rock*."

Gordon goes on to reflect on the book after more than three decades had passed:

"Black Rock is an example," he writes, "of that rather rare thing in writing, a successful novel with a purpose. *Black Rock* is really a phenomenon in a way, indeed in several ways. I am too far on in life now, I hope, and moreover I have seen too much of the real things in life to lay myself open to the charge of egotism if I speak frankly about Ralph Connor and his books. When I sent those first three articles to Jim MacDonald I had no more thought of a book in my mind than I have now of flying to the North Pole. Slightly less in fact, for I should dearly like to encircle the pole in an airplane.

"My sole purpose was to awaken my church in Eastern Canada to the splendor of the mighty religious adventure being attempted by the missionary pioneers in the Canada beyond the Great Lakes by writing a brief sketch of the things which as clerk of the biggest presbytery in the world I had come to know by personal experience."

When MacDonald received Gordon's three-chapter fictional "sketch" of life in the West, he found no name attached as author. He promptly wrote his friend, asking him what to use, his own or a pen name.

Gordon thought and thought, trying to come up with something which would be appropriate. At length, while sitting at his desk, his eyes chanced upon the heading on the note paper he was then using as secretary of the British Canadian Northwest Mission, which had been shortened on the stationery into the form "Brit. Can. Nor. West Mission." The two abbreviations next to one another—*Can. Nor.*—caught his eye, he circled them with his pencil, and went to wire MacDonald the message—"Sign article Cannor."

The telegraph operator, however, had never heard of such as being as "Cannor" and took it upon himself to change the message to read Connor. MacDonald himself added the first name, and thus was born to the world the pseudonym "Ralph Connor."

The first three chapters were printed in the *Westminster Magazine*, MacDonald wrote asking for three more, and then followed a third set of three. Whereupon MacDonald wrote his friend saying, "We will make a book of this." And armed with his nine chapters MacDonald went to New York to find a publisher.

But no one was interested. It was "too religious," they said, "too temperance." It would never sell.

But Jim MacDonald thought he knew better. He determined that he would publish the book in Canada, and publish it himself if he had to!

It was a daring venture. Few novels had ever been published in Canada at that time, but MacDonald was convinced that the project had merit and decided to try it. He was advised by several leading Canadian booksellers to risk an edition of 800 copies. But he decided to "go the whole hog," as he wrote Gordon, and publish a first edition of 1,000 copies. *Black Rock* was thus released in 1898.

The risk element in the publication of Ralph Connor's books vanished almost immediately. An American publisher was found through a young editor who had followed the chapters in *Westminster*. They were eager by this time to publish an American edition.

They did so. In the span of a year several hundred thousand copies had been sold in hardback. Within a very short time "Ralph Connor" was one of America's best selling authors.

Black Rock, released in 1898, became so immensely popular that it was followed the following year with *The Sky Pilot*, and thereafter Connor continued to write novel after novel, about one a year, throughout the remainder of his professional life. In a sense he carried on two careers: Charles Gordon, the Winnipeg minister and national religious figure; and Ralph Connor, the intriguing wanderer about the frontier of Western Canada whose travels and adventures—a curious mixture of fiction and fact—were immortalized forever in the novels bearing his name. Gordon liked the name *Ralph Connor* from the start, did not try to hide his own presence behind the pen name, and in time came to answer equally to either epithet, feeling as if he were two men in one—as in fact he was.[1]

The Canadian West, the Scottish Highlanders who had emigrated to this land across the sea, the missionary adventures of young pioneers of the gospel, a love for the out of doors and the great mountain country, and a passion to raise up young men and women as ministers and missionaries of the gospel to the world's frontiers wherever they might be—these were all significant threads of Connor's life and interest, and all come out in his books. It was in hopes of inspiring others to leave comfort behind and respond to "the call" of God to go west, which initially motivated Gordon's pen, and this theme runs throughout several of his stories. The combination of exciting story and adventure, along with compelling characters who stood firm for purity and Godly truth, won Connor many thousands of readers who might

[1]Much of the information here, as well as the quotations, are taken from *Postscript to Adventure: The Autobiography of Ralph Connor* by Charles William Gordon, Canadian Bookman Pubs., 1930, pp. 146-150.

otherwise never have indulged in novels. And indeed, many of these same readers staunchly affirmed that they were not fiction at all, notwithstanding Connor's natural storytelling ability, for they knew that "a meenister couldna tell lies."

It is precisely this fascinating blend between reality and fiction, between characters of his own invention and real people he knew, that makes Connor's books so wonderfully compelling. By his own admission, they are clearly autobiographical, drawing, as they do, from his own days of youth. However, they are not strictly autobiographical. In other words, though Ralph Connor himself is a player on the stage of both *Black Rock* and *The Sky Pilot,* and though the books are narrated in the first person, and though in them Connor uses his real name, the Connor of the book is not really the Connor of history. Connor the writer employs the fascinating literary device of intruding himself into the narrative as an observer to what goes on, even as an observer to his *own* part in the story. For though Connor the narrator expresses skepticism as to the claims of young Thomas Skyler of *The Sky Pilot,* in reality Skyler is a fictional characterization of aspects of Connor (the writer's) own days as a green young missionary. And no doubt this same dichotomy exists between the Connor who narrates *Black Rock* and Ralph Connor himself, for whom Jim Craig might well have been a symbol. Of course these are things about which we can merely speculate. But it makes the books all the more interesting on several levels.

Similarly, since "Connor" is a pseudonym, Gordon as a writer was free to let his Ralph Connor move throughout Canada with great freedom, writing fiction, telling stories, blending facts and real people with a great yarn-spinning ability, but always telling "the Truth." Thus Connor, as a writer, as a narrator who moved in and out of stories observing life's drama, now in Black Rock, now in Swan Creek, now in Toronto, now in Glengarry, became almost a mystical, shadowy figure with a character all his own. You could never tell, it seemed, when this "Ralph Connor" might pop up—he could be in your midst any time without warning—writing, observing, drawing sketches about life from the people he met, then chronicling what he saw. The touching scene in *Black Rock* where Sandy leads his friends through an informal "Bible study" on the straw floor of the stable, serves almost as a parable to the perspective of Connor's writing style. For where is the fictional Connor while Sandy is speaking? Outside the stable, peeking through a crack in the logs, watching but not speaking, observing, then writing of what he has seen. All the while the men inside sitting on the dirt floor know nothing of his presence. Ralph Connor, then, is a writer of stories, a narrator of those stories, and even an actor within his own stories, though none of the three are necessarily to be equated with Charles Gordon himself.

Because of all this, the Foreword to the first edition of *Black Rock* by then well-known George Adam Smith takes on a mysteriously beguiling note: "I think I have met 'Ralph Connor.' Indeed, I am sure I have—once in a canoe on the Red River, once on the Assinaboine, and twice or three times on the prairies of the West. That was not the name he gave me, of course."

The literary technique of intruding himself into the story, is thus used for maximum effect by Ralph Connor, whose very presence becomes a subplot to the story itself, and provides an impact not possible without such a "first hand" account.

For these and many reasons, Ralph Connor is an author I am excited about. His works are, in my opinion, both historically and spiritually significant. It is my sincere hope and prayer that you will enjoy and be blessed by this new and updated edition of *Black Rock* which I have done for Sunrise Books, Publishers. It has been retitled *Jim Craig's Battle For Black Rock* as Volume 1 in the Sunrise "Stories of Yesteryear" series.

Michael Phillips

FOREWORD

I think I have met "Ralph Connor." Indeed, I am sure I have—once in a canoe on the Red River, once on the Assinaboine, and twice or three times on the prairies of the West.

That was not the name he gave me, of course. But if I am right, it covers one of the most honest and genial of the strong characters that are fighting the devil and doing good work for men all over the world. He has seen with his own eyes the life he describes in this book, and has himself, for some years of hard and lonely toil, assisted in the good influences which he traces among its wild and often hopeless conditions. He writes with the freshness and accuracy of an eyewitness, with the style (as I think his readers will allow) of a real artist, and with the tenderness and hopefulness of a man not only of faith, but of experience, who has seen in fulfillment the ideals for which he lives.

The life to which he takes us, though far off and very strange to our tame minds, is the life of our brothers. Into the Northwest of Canada the young men of Great Britain and Ireland have been pouring (I was told) sometimes at the rate of 48,000 a year. Our brothers who left home yesterday —our hearts cannot but follow them.

With these pages Ralph Connor enables our eyes and our minds to follow too. Nor do I think there is anyone who shall read this book and not find also that his conscience is quickened. There is a warfare appointed unto man upon earth, and its struggles are nowhere more intense, nor the victories of the strong, nor the succors brought to the fallen, more heroic, than on the fields described in this volume.

Professor George Adam Smith, LL.D., 1900

PREFACE

The story of this book is true, and chief of the failures in the making of the book is this, that it is not all the truth. The light is not bright enough, the shadow is not black enough to give a true picture of that bit of Western life of which the writer was some small part. The men of the book are still there in the mines and lumber camps of the mountains, fighting out that eternal fight for manhood, strong, clean, God-conquered. And, when the west winds blow, to the open ear the sounds of battle come, telling the fortunes of the fight.

Because a man's life is all he has, and because the only hope of the brave young West lies in its men, this story is told. It may be that the tragic pity of a broken life may move some to pray, and that that divine power there is in a single brave heart to summon forth hope and courage may move some to fight. If so, the tale is not told in vain.

C.W.G.
Winnipeg, Canada, 1898

Sandy was reading the undying story of the Prodigal.

1.

CHRISTMAS EVE IN A LUMBER CAMP

It was due to a mysterious dispensation of Providence, and a good deal to Leslie Graeme, that I found myself in the heart of the Selkirks for Christmas Eve at the end of the year 1882.

I had been sent to western Canada by the railroad to paint scenes of what was then viewed as the raw, untamed land west of the Rockies. My pictures, it was hoped, would help raise support for this new "Iron Horse" to expand all the way to the Pacific. I had been there some time, and knew the region of the Selkirk mountains in southeast British Columbia rather well. But my work was nearly concluded, and it had been my plan to spend the Christmas season far away in Toronto with friends.

Leslie Graeme, however, changed all that.

Discovering me early in December in the village of Black Rock, with my equipment and bags all packed and waiting for the stagecoach to start for the Landing some thirty miles away, he bore down upon me with forces I was powerless to resist. I found myself recovering from my surprise only after we had gone in his lumber sleigh some six miles on our way to his camp up in the mountains above the village. I was both surprised and delighted to see him, though I could hardly allow him to see how much. A friend like Graeme could make one forget an exciting and cosmopolitan city like Toronto in no time, and I hardly wondered to find that his old power over me was still there. In the old college days he could always make me do what he liked. He was so handsome and reckless, brilliant at his studies, fearless on the athletic field, and with a power of fascination as would extract the heart out of a wheelbarrow, as our friend Barney Lundy used to say.

And thus it was that I found myself three weeks later, on the afternoon of December 24, still at Graeme's Lumber Camp #2, standing gazing about me in the silence of Christmas Eve, curious that I could have allowed my plans to become altered so suddenly. But I did not regret the change, for it had been an eye-opening three weeks. Yet there would be much more to come, which I could not at this moment anticipate.

For still I had not met Craig.

I would meet him later that evening, however. For having a second time determined to go, it was Craig whom my friend had arranged for me to ride down the mountain with, in readiness for the morning's stage. I would soon find these plans no easier to keep than my original ones earlier in the month.

The camp stood in a little clearing, and consisted of three long, low shanties with smaller shacks near them, all built of heavy, unhewn logs, with a door and window in each. The grub camp, with cookshed attached, stood in the middle of the clearing. At a little distance were the sleeping quarters with the office built against it, and about a hundred yards away on the other side of the clearing stood the stables, and near them the smithy. The mountains rose grandly on every side, throwing up their great peaks into the sky. The clearing in which the camp stood had been cut out of a dense pine forest that filled the valley and climbed halfway up the mountainsides, then frayed out in scattered and stunted trees.

It was one of those wonderful Canadian winter days, when I stood reflecting on this place that had for three weeks now been my temporary home—a bright day, with a touch of sharpness in the air that did not chill but instead warmed the blood. The men were up in the woods. The shrill scream of a blue jay flashing across the sky, the impudent chatter of the red squirrel from on top of the grub camp, and the pert chirp of the whiskey jack, with the long, lone cry of the wolf far down the valley, only made the silence felt the more. Leaving this place would be hard, I said to myself, but I had already spent far more time here than the two or three days I had originally planned on.

As I stood drinking in with all my soul the glorious beauty and the silence of mountain and forest, with the Christmas feeling stealing into me, Graeme came out from his office, caught sight of me, and called out, "Glorious Christmas weather, old chap!" Then, coming nearer, he added, "Must you really go tomorrow?"

"I'm afraid so," I replied, knowing all too well that the Christmas feeling was upon him too.

"I wish I were going with you," he said quietly.

I turned eagerly and was about to try to persuade him to do so, but at the look on his face the words died on my lips. I knew we were both thinking of the calamities in his life which had sent him West in the first place. I could only throw my arm over his shoulder and stand silently beside him. A sudden jingle of bells roused him, and, giving himself a little shake, he exclaimed, "There are the boys coming home."

Before many more minutes the sleigh had arrived and the camp was filled with men talking, laughing, and joking like light-hearted boys.

"They are a little wild tonight," said Graeme, "and

tomorrow they'll paint Black Rock red."

It did not take long for everyone to get washed up, and soon all were standing about waiting impatiently for the Cook's signal—supper tonight was supposed to be some special kind of feast. All at once the sound of bells drew their attention to a light sleigh drawn by a buckskin bronco coming down the hill at a rapid pace.

"The preacher, I'll bet, by his driving," said one of the men.

"He's got a nose for the turkey!" said Blaney, a good-natured, jovial Irishman.

"More likely for pay day," added Keefe in a sarcastic grumble. The black-browed, villainous-looking man was a fellow countryman of Blaney's, and his great friend.

Big Sandy McNaughton, a Canadian Highlander from Glengarry, rose up in anger at the words. "Bill Keefe, you keep your dirty tongue off the minister! And as for your pay, it's little he sees of it, or anyone else around here, except Mike Slavin in his saloon."

Keefe jumped up with a curse. A wiry little French Canadian by the name of Baptiste, Sandy's sworn ally and devoted admirer, sprang to the big Scotsman's side, and it looked as if Christmas eve was about to be ushered in with a fight. But before it had the chance to go any further, a harsh voice said in a low, savage tone, "Stop your row, you fools! Settle it if you want to somewhere else." I turned and was amazed to see old man Nelson, who was very seldom moved to such outbursts of speech.

There was a look of scorn on his hard, iron-gray face, and with it such a settled fierceness as made me an instant believer in the tales I had heard of his deadly fights in the mines in his younger days. But before another word could be spoken, the minister drove up and called out in a cheery voice—

"Merry Christmas, boys! Hello, Sandy. Comment ca va, Baptiste? How are you tonight, Mr. Graeme?"

"Good—nice to see you. Let me introduce my friend, Mr. Connor, sometime medical student, artist, hunter, and tramp at large, but not a bad sort."

"A man to be envied," said the minister, smiling. "I am glad to know any friend of Mr. Graeme's."

I liked Mr. Craig from the first. He had good eyes that looked straight out at you, a clean-cut strong face well set on his shoulders, and an altogether upstanding and manly bearing. There was certainly nothing of the weakling about him as, in some circles, is occasionally associated with men of the cloth. He insisted on going to the stables with Sandy to see his bronco Dandy put up.

"Decent fellow," said Graeme, "but though he's good enough to his horse, it's Sandy that's on his mind now."

"Does he come out often?" I asked. "I mean, are you part of his parish?"

"I imagine he thinks so. But a dandy bunch of parishioners we make for any man."

He paused, apparently in thought, then went on, "Take Sandy for instance. He would knock Keefe's head off as a kind of religious exercise. But tomorrow Keefe will be sober and Sandy drunk. And the drunker he is the better Presbyterian he'll think himself, to the preacher's disgust." Then after another pause, he added, "But it is not for me to throw rocks at Sandy. I may not be the same kind of fool, but I am a fool in several other ways."

Then the cook came out and beat a tattoo on the bottom of a dish pan. Baptiste answered with a yell and the men filed inside. Though everyone was keenly hungry after their hard day's work, no man would demean himself to hurry to his place at the table. At the further end of the room was a big fireplace, and from the door to the fireplace extended the long board tables, covered with platters of turkey not too scientifically carved, dishes of potatoes, bowls of applesauce, slabs of butter, pies, and smaller dishes distributed at regular intervals. Two lanterns hanging from the roof, and a row of candles stuck into a wall on either side, cast a dim light over the scene.

There was a moment's silence, then at a nod from Graeme, Mr. Craig rose and said, "I don't know how you feel about it men, but to me this looks good enough to be thankful for."

"Fire ahead," called out a voice quite respectfully, and the minister bowed his head and said—

"For Christ the Lord who came to save us, for all the love and goodness we have known, and for these your gifts to us this Christmas night, our Father, make us thankful. Amen."

For the next quarter of an hour not a word was spoken. The occasion was far too solemn and moments too precious for anything so empty as words. But when the white piles of bread and the brown piles of turkey had for a second time vanished, and after the last pie had disappeared, there came a pause and a hush of expectancy, whereupon the cook and his assistant, each bearing aloft a huge, blazing pudding, came forth from the kitchen.

"Hooray!" yelled Blaney. "Up wi' ye all!"

Mr. Craig was the first to respond, jumping up, taking his place behind the Irishman, and calling out, "Squad, fall in! Quick march!" and in a moment every man was in the procession as the pudding made its way round the tables.

"Strike it up, Baptiste!" shouted Blaney, and away went the Frenchman in a rollicking French song with the English chorus—

> *"Then blow, ye winds, in the morning,*
> *Blow, ye winds, ay oh!*
> *Blow, ye winds, in the morning,*
> *Blow, blow, blow."*

And at each *blow* every boot came down with a thump on the plank floor that shook the solid roof. After the second round, Mr. Craig jumped upon the bench and called out—

"Three cheers for Billy the Cook!"

In the silence following the cheers, Baptiste was heard to say, "Bon, dat's make me feel lak eating dat puddin' all up meself."

"Batchees," remonstrated Sandy, "ye've got more stomach than manners."

The men quickly resumed their places, and before long the pudding had been done away with like everything else.

After a time the tables were cleared and pushed back to the wall, and pipes were produced. In all positions suggestive of comfort the men disposed themselves in a wide circle about the fire, which now roared and crackled up the great chimney. The lumberman's hour of bliss had arrived. Even old man Nelson looked a shade less melancholy than usual as he sat alone, well away from the fire, smoking steadily and silently.

When the pipes had been smoked, filled a second time, and were again well in progress, one of the men took down a violin from the wall and handed it to Lachlan Campbell. There were two brothers Campbell just out from Argyll in Scotland, typical Highlanders: Lachlan was dark, silent, melancholy, with the face of a mystic; and Angus was redhaired, quick, impulsive, and devoted to his brother.

After much protestation, Lachlan took up the violin, and, in response to the call from all sides, struck up *Lord MacDonald's Reel*. In a moment the floor was filled with dancers, whooping and clapping their hands in the wildest manner. Then Baptiste did the *Red River Jig*, a most intricate series of steps, while the men looked on and kept time to the music with hands and feet.

When the jig was finished, Sandy called for *Lochaber No More*, but Campbell said, "No. I cannot play that tonight. Mr. Craig will play."

Craig took the violin, and at the first note I knew he was no ordinary player. I did not recognize the music, but it was soft and thrilling, and got in by the heart, till everyone was thinking the tenderest and saddest thoughts.

After he had played ten or fifteen minutes, he gave Campbell his violin, saying, "Now *Lochaber*, Lachlan."

Without a word Lachlan began, not *Lochaber*—he was not ready for that yet—but *The Flowers o' the Forest* and from that wandered through *Auld Robin Gray* and *The Land o' the Leal* and so got at last to that most soul-subduing of Scottish laments, *Lochaber No More*. At the first strain, his brother, who had thrown himself on some blankets in front of the fire, turned over on his face and pretended to be asleep. Sandy McNaughton took his pipe out of his mouth and sat up straight and stiff, staring into the night, and Graeme, beyond the fire, drew in a short, sharp breath. We had often sat, Graeme and I, in our student days —like many a Scotsman to whom the music was the most poignant reminder of our heritage in the drawing room at his family home, listening to his minister father wailing out *Lochaber* on his bagpipes, and I well knew that the nostalgic minor strains were now eating their way into his soul.

Over and over the Highlander played his lament. He had long since forgotten us, and was seeing visions and hills and lochs and glens of his faraway native land, and making us, too, see strange things out of the dim past. I glanced at old man Nelson and was surprised to see the look in his eyes. I almost wished Campbell would stop, for the music was working powerfully on the hearts of the men gathered there. Mr. Craig caught my eye, and, stepping over to Campbell, held out his hand for the violin. Lingeringly the Highlander drew out the last prolonged strain, then silently gave the minister his instrument.

Without a moment's pause, and while the spell of *Lochaber* was still upon us, the minister with exquisite skill fell into the refrain of that simple and beautiful camp-meeting hymn, *The Sweet By and By*. He played the verse through once, then softly sang the refrain. After the first verse, the men joined in the chorus, at first somewhat timidly. But by the time the third verse was reached they were singing with throats full open, *We shall meet on that beautiful shore.* When I looked at Nelson, the eager light that had flickered upon him before was gone out of his eyes, and in its place was something which seemed to say that he had no part in this new music.

After the singing had ceased, Mr. Craig played again the refrain, more and more softly and slowly. Then, laying the violin on Campbell's knees, he drew from his pocket his little Bible, and said—

"Men, with Graeme's permission, I want to read you something this Christmas Eve. You will all have heard it before, but you will like it none the less for that."

His voice was soft, but clear and penetrating, and he began to read the story of the angels and the shepherds and the Babe. As he read, a slight motion of the hand or a glance of the eye made us see the drama of the moment. The wonder, the timid joy, the tenderness, the mystery of it all, were borne in upon us in a very simple but overpowering way. At length he closed the book, and in the same low, clear voice went on to tell us how, in his home years ago, he used to stand on Christmas Eve listening to his mother tell him the story.

"Her words would make me see the shepherds and the sheep nearby, and—oh, how the sudden burst of glory made my heart jump!"

"I used to be a little afraid of the angels," he went on, "because another boy told me they were ghosts. But my mother told me better, and I wasn't afraid anymore. And the Baby, the dear little baby—we all love a baby—"

I could see that hard old Nelson was hanging on every word, as if he had been a child again.

"—I used to wonder what things swaddling clothes were. Oh, it was all so real and so beautiful!" He paused, and I could hear the men breathing.

"But one Christmas Eve," he went on, "there was no

31

one to tell me the story, and I grew to forget it, and I went away to college and learned to think that it was only a child's tale and was not for real men. Then bad days came to me, and I began to lose my grip on myself, on life, on hope, on goodness, till one black Christmas, in the slums of a faraway city, when I had given up on life and the devil's arms were about me, I heard the story again. And as I listened, with a bitter ache in my heart, I suddenly found myself peeking under the shepherd's arms with a child's wonder at the Baby in the straw. Then it came over me like great waves, that His name was Jesus, because he should *save* men from their sins. The waves kept beating upon my ears, and before I knew it I was calling out, 'Can He save me?' It was in a little mission meeting on one of the side streets, and hearing the Christmas story gave me such a new hope in my soul."

He stopped quite short. Graeme, poor old chap, was gazing at him with a sad yearning in his dark eyes. He had certainly heard the tale time and again, yet now, I suspected, was going through his own time of doubt. Big Sandy was sitting very stiff and staring harder than ever into the fire. Baptiste was almost trembling. Blaney was openly wiping the tears away. But the face that held my eyes was that of the old man Nelson.

The minister went on. "I didn't mean to tell you all this, men. It all came back to me like a rush. But every word I have told you is true. And I can tell you this—what He did for me He can do for any man, and it makes no difference what in life's behind you. Without Him you'll never be the men you want to be, and you'll never get the better of the things that are keeping some of you now from going back home. For you know you'll never go back till you're the men you want to be." Then adding, almost as if to himself, he said, "Jesus! He shall save His people from their sins...Let us pray."

Graeme leaned forward with his face in his hands, Baptiste and Blaney dropped on their knees. Sandy, the Campbells, and some others, stood up. Old man Nelson held his eyes steadily on the minister.

The look on Nelson's face was one of mute and pitiful horror. But during the prayer the face changed, and it seemed to settle into a resolve of some sort—stern, almost gloomy, as of a man with his last chance before him.

After the prayer Mr. Craig invited the men to a Christmas dinner next day in Black Rock. "And because you are an independent lot, we'll charge you half a dollar for dinner and the evening show." Then leaving a bundle of magazines and illustrated papers on the table—a godsend to the men in this faraway place—he said good-bye and went out.

Since I was to go with him, I put my things into the sleigh and then jumped in, while Craig said good-bye to Graeme, who seemed to have been especially struck by the events of the evening. As he climbed in, the minister turned to Sandy, who had been doing his best to steady Dandy, and said, "Come and see me first thing."

"Ay! I'll see ye, Mr. Craig," he replied earnestly.

And with that we were off across the snow. But hardly had we gone fifty feet when Dandy took a sudden turn, nearly upsetting us. A man stepped out from the shadows. It was old man Nelson. He came straight to the sleigh, and, seeming to ignore my presence altogether, said—

"Craig, are you dead sure of this, what you was telling us? Will it work?"

"Do you mean," replied Craig, "can Jesus save you from your sins and make a man of you?"

The old man nodded, keeping his eyes on the other's face.

"Dead sure! Here is His message to you: 'The Son of Man came to seek and to save that which was lost.' "

"To me, you say?"

"You, and all like you—and me! For we are all lost without Him."

33

"But you don't know me, Mr. Craig. I left my baby fifteen years ago because—"

But Nelson did not finish the sentence.

"Stop," interrupted the minister. "Don't tell me. At least not tonight. Tell Him who knows it all now, and who never betrays a secret. Have it out with Him. Don't be afraid to trust Him."

Nelson looked at him, with his face almost quivering, and said in a husky voice, "If this is no good, it's hell for me. This is my last hope."

"If it's no good," replied Craig, "it's hell for all of us."

The old man straightened himself up, looked at the stars, then back at Craig, then at me, and, drawing a deep breath said, "I'll try Him." As he was turning away the minister touched him on the arm and said quietly, "Keep an eye on Sandy tomorrow."

Nelson nodded, then we began to move on again through the night.

Before we took the next turn, I looked back and saw what brought a lump into my throat. It was old man Nelson on his knees in the snow, with his hands lifted upward to the stars. And I wondered if there was any One above the stars, and nearer than the stars, who could see.

Then the trees hid him from my sight.

2.

THE BATTLE FOR BLACK ROCK BEGINS

I have seen many unusual Christmas celebrations through the years, but that wild Black Rock Christmas of 1882 stands out from among them as the strangest of all. While I was still reveling in the drowsy stage before coming fully awake, Mr. Craig, who had been kind enough to put me up for the night, walked abruptly into the room announced breakfast, and then added:

"Hope you're in good shape, because we have our work cut out for us today."

"Good morning!" I replied, still half asleep. But as I came more fully awake his words sunk in, and I added, "But what do you mean? My stage leaves in a couple of hours."

"You can't leave now," he answered with a friendly grin. "The devil's about...closing in on all sides," he added with much emphasis.

Sitting bolt upright in my bed, I looked anxiously around.

"No need for alarm!" said Craig, laughing. "He's not after you particularly—at least not today. But he will be making the rounds today in good style, that I can tell you."

"And what particular shape will the scoundrel be known by today?" I asked, rising.

He pulled out a show bill—a leaflet advertising the day's festivities at Mike Slavin's saloon.

"Gaudy and effective, is it not?" he said.

The items announced were designed to be suitably attractive to rough-and-tumble miners and lumbermen, hundreds and even thousands of miles from home. The Frisco Opera Company was to produce what was billed as a "screaming farce," *The Gay and Giddy Dude;* after which there was to be a "Grand Ball" during which some "lovely ladies," dubbed the Kalifornia High Kickers, were to do some fancy figures; the whole thing to be followed by a big supper with two free drinks to every man and one to the lady. All this for the insignificant sum of two dollars.

As I eyed the bill, Craig must have seen from my expression that the whole thing did not strike me so dreadfully as it apparently did him.

"It's not the play and the dancers," he said. "It's the drinks! That's all Slavin wants—to get the men drinking. Once that starts, the whole thing's lost!"

"Can't you go one better?" I said. "What about your own dinner and entertainment?"

For the first time since I had met the man, a look, almost of momentary defeat, seemed to cross over Craig's face like a shadow.

"I've got no entertainment," he said.

"But last night you said—"

"I know. I said the men would get dinner and a show. Well, they'll get the dinner all right. But as for the show —that's where I hoped you might come in."

"Me?"

"Without some help, I'm beat. What can I do against the high hickers and a dance, not to mention the free drinks?" he almost groaned. "The miners and lumbermen will have ten thousand dollars in their pockets, and every dollar burning holes right through them. And Slavin and his gang will get most of it. All this time I've been fighting it, but some of the men seem lost as ever."

"But what can I do? I'm leaving town today."

He sighed, then said, "I know. Of course, you're right." Then he turned and made for the door. "But you must have breakfast first," he added in a subdued tone. "You'll find a tub in the kitchen. Don't be afraid to splash. It is the best I have to offer you."

The tub sounded inviting, and before many minutes had passed I was in a delightful glow—the effect of cold water and a rough towel, and that consciousness of virtue that comes to a man who has had courage to face his cold bath on a winter morning.

The breakfast was well laid. A small pine Christmas tree stood in the center of the table in an iron pot.

"Well, now, this looks good," I said, surveying the table with delight, "porridge, beefsteak, potatoes, toast, and marmalade."

"I hope you will enjoy it all," my host replied.

There was not much talk over our meal. Mr. Craig was evidently preoccupied and as glum as his politeness would allow. Slavin's apparent victory weighed upon his spirits.

After about ten minutes he suddenly burst out, "I won't stand for it! Something must be done! Last Christmas this town was for two weeks, as one of the miners said, 'a little suburb of hell.' It was terrible! At the end of it all, one young fellow was found dead in his shack, and twenty or more crawled back to the camps, leaving their three months' pay with Slavin and his men. I won't stand for it!"

He turned almost fiercely on me. There was fire in his eyes. "What's to be done?" he demanded.

His outburst took me rather aback. I had made it my practice never to trouble myself with this sort of thing. I occupied myself fully in keeping out of difficulty, and always had allowed others the same privilege. I wasn't use thinking of myself as my brother's keeper. Thus Craig, who apparently regarded himself as exactly that, did not appreciate my words. I ventured the consolation that he had done his part, that he had spoken words of truth about the season to them the night before, and that a spree more or less wouldn't make such difference to such men as these. But the next moment I wished my words had been more carefully chosen, for he swiftly turned toward me, his eyes ablaze with righteous indignation, and his words came like a torrent.

"God forgive you those heartless words! Do you know—"

He paused, seemed to think with himself for a brief moment, then continued.

"—But no; you don't know what you are saying. You don't know that these men have been struggling for dear life for the past three months to crawl out of a fearful pit of drink. The poor chaps! How can you know that some of them have wives, most of them mothers and sisters, in the East or across the sea in Scotland, for whose sake they are slaving here. They have come because there is hard work and money here—work which they couldn't find at home. Many of the miners are hoping to save enough to bring their families to this homeless place. The rest are hoping to make enough to go back with something in their pockets. Why, there's Nixon—a miner, splendid fellow; has been here for two years and drawing the highest pay of anyone. Twice he has been in sight of his heaven, for he can't speak of his wife and babies without breaking up; twice he had had enough to send for them, and twice that son of the devil—that's Scripture, mind you—Slavin, got him and 'rolled' him as the boys say, and left him penniless. He went back to the mines broken in body and heart. He says this is his third and last chance. If Slavin gets him again, his wife and little children will never see him on earth, or in heaven either for that matter. There is Sandy, too, and all the rest."

He stopped again. By now the anger in his voice had been replaced by a great anguish. It was clear he not only hated the evils of drink, but loved these wild Western men whom he regarded as his charge.

"And," he added, in a lower tone with a touch of pathos in his voice, "the most important thing of all—this is the day the Saviour came to the world."

He paused, and then with a sad little smile, said, "But I'm sorry I spoke harshly. I don't want to abuse you. After all, you are my guest."

Now it was my turn to be silent. His words had penetrated into my soul. Perhaps—but who can tell about such things?—his heartfelt little talk the night before about the true meaning of Christmas had softened something in me, made me more receptive. Perhaps it was the day itself, for who can escape thoughts of reflection on Christmas?

Whatever the reason, his intense blazing earnestness, the compassion in his eyes toward these men—it all made me feel uncomfortably small. He was right—I didn't know what I was saying! I had no idea what a big difference a little "spree" would make.

But even more than this, his words forced me to ask myself when I had ever done anything for anyone else. Maybe I hadn't been all that bad a sort. Perhaps I had allowed everyone I met their freedom. But was that enough? When had I, for no other reason than because it was the right thing to do, put someone else's needs ahead of my own?

I couldn't think of a single time.

"I...I don't exactly know what to say," I half stammered. "Please—go on with whatever you want to say. You were right...I had no idea what I was saying."

"It's just that these men—and most of them are all right underneath—they deserve better. They're trying hard, and they want better. But when the smell of drink floats under their noses, they just can't help themselves. That's why I had hoped to do something for them today. I suppose I was foolish to announce it like I did."

Suddenly my plan to catch the stage seemed rather insignificant. There was another moment or two of silence, during which I found myself thinking hard.

"Well, what do we have to offer?" I asked finally, surprised at the resolve which had come over me.

"Now it's my turn to ask what *you* mean?" said Craig, looking up at me across the table, a faint gleam of hope in his eye. "Explain yourself—what do you mean by asking me what *we* have to offer?"

"There will be another stage through in a few days," I said. Then I smiled; I could not help myself. Without knowing it, the preacher had thrown out a challenge I couldn't refuse. But even more, the man himself attracted me; and I found myself unwilling to leave before I saw how this drama was going to turn out.

3.
PLANS

The remainder of the morning Craig spent planning how to counter Slavin's men later that afternoon. He made me feel that I was helping him, but once the fire was back in his eyes he was a wellspring of enthusiasm all his own.

"I can offer dinner and music," he said, once we had our breakfast things cleared away and were reseated at his table. "And perhaps a magic lantern slide show. The men always like pictures of far away places, especially home! We might be able to fill in time for two hours. But I don't know how to beat the dance and the high kicking women!"

"Have you nothing new or sensational?" I asked.

He shook his head.

"No kind of show? No dog show? Snake charmers?"

"Slavin has a monopoly on all the snakes," he said with a wry grin. "There was an old chap who did a Punch-and-Judy puppet show here last year. But he died. Whisky again!"

"What happened to his show—his puppet theater and props?"

"The Black Rock Hotel man took it for board and whis-

41

key bill. He still has it, I suppose."

I did not much relish the idea, but I was in it with him by now. So I ventured:

"I used to run a Punch-and-Judy in an amateur way in college."

He sprang to his feet with a yell.

"You mean it? That might be just what we need! The miner chaps, mostly English and Welsh, went mad over the poor old showman last year. They made him so wealthy that in sheer gratitude he drank himself to death."

"Well," I said, "if I'm going to do this, we'll need posters first. They have their show bills. So we'll need our own announcements."

He disappeared into another part of his small cabin, and returned in a few moments with several large sheets of paper.

It was fortunate that drawing was my vocation—at present at least, or in any event more a vocation than puppeteering—and after two hours' hard work I had half a dozen pictorial show bills done in rather striking colors and action designs. Considering the circumstances, they were not bad even if I do say so myself.

The turkey dinner, the slide show, the Punch-and-Judy theater were all on the posters, with a huge crowd shown in gaping delight. On the top and bottom were a few explanatory words, emphasizing the advantages to be gained by attending this marvelous entertainment and Christmas meal.

Craig was delighted, and proceeded to perfect the rest of his plans.

He had some half dozen young men, four young ladies, and eight or ten married women he could depend on for help. He would organize them into a vigilance committee charged with the duty of preventing any lumberman and miners from getting into Slavin's saloon.

"The critical moments will be immediately before and after dinner, and then again when the show is over," he explained. "The first two crises must be left to the care of you and Punch-and-Judy. I'm not yet sure what I can arrange for after the show."

But I could tell he had something on his mind, for he added, heading for the door, "I shall see Mrs. Mavor."

"Who is Mrs. Mavor?" I asked.

But he was already gone. I marveled at his vision, his spirit, his determination. He was a born fighter, and in no time he put the fighting spirit into us all. I found myself already framing the story I would later recount to my father about the conquering of Black Rock.

The western-style sports of the day were to begin at two o'clock. By noon everything was ready. After lunch I was having a quiet smoke in Craig's cabin when he rushed in.

"What's up?" I asked.

"Slavin, just now. The miners are coming into town and he will have them in tow in half an hour. Can you put on a quick show?"

"I suppose I must," I replied, rising. It had been years, and I was not in the least confident about my abilities.

"You're not half a bad fellow," he replied with a smile. "I'll get the ladies to furnish coffee inside the tent. You can furnish them intellectual nourishment in front with dear old Punch-and-Judy."

He immediately sent a boy with a bell to go around the village announcing: "Punch-and-Judy in front of the Christmas tent beside the church."

When the modest crowd had assembled, I began my act, and for three quarters of an hour I shrieked and sweated in that tiny little pen. But it was almost worth it to hear the shouts of approval and laughter that greeted my performance. It was a cold day, and all the more so for the onlookers standing around watching. So the crowd was quite ready to respond when Punch, at the conclusion of his antics, stepped out of character and invited all inside the tent for the hot coffee which Judy had ordered.

In they trooped, and the first round appeared to be ours.

No sooner were the miners safely engaged with their coffee than I heard a great noise of bells and of men shouting. I went out to the street and saw that the men from the lumber camp were coming in. Two huge sleighs, decorated with ribbons and spruce boughs, each drawn by a four-horse team gaily adorned, were filled with some fifty men, singing and shouting with all their might, and coming down the hill road at a full gallop over the snow.

Round the corner they swung, dashed at full speed across the bridge and down the street, and to the great admiration of all the onlookers, made the circuit around the block and finally pulled up.

Slavin and several others sauntered up good-naturedly as the men were getting out, and made themselves agreeable to Sandy and those who were helping to unhitch his team.

"Don't trouble yourself, Slavin," said Sandy coolly. "Batchees and me and the boys can look after them fine."

Slavin, and the others who heard, perfectly understood this rejection of hospitality.

"Dat's too bad, eh?" said Baptiste, winking at Slavin. "And he's got good money in his pocket too."

The boys laughed. Slavin, joining in with them, turned away with Keefe and Blaney. But by the wicked look in his eye, I knew he was playing Brer Rabbit, and lying low for now.

Just then Mr. Craig came up.

"Hello, boys!" he called out. "You're too late for the puppet show, but just in time for hot coffee and doughnuts!"

"Dat's first rate," said Baptiste heartily. "Where you keep them?"

"In the tent next to the church there. The miners are all inside already."

"Bad new for the shantymen, eh, Sandy?" said the little Frenchman.

44

A group of the men, led by Baptiste, headed off toward the church.

"There was a clothes-basket full of doughnuts and a boiler of coffee left as I passed just now," Craig called after them. "But leave some for the rest!"

He walked up to Sandy. "Care to join us?" he said.

But Sandy would not leave the horses till they were carefully rubbed down, blanketed, and fed, for he was entered in the four-horse race later in the day and he wanted to do his best to win. In addition, he scorned to hurry himself for anything so unimportant as eating.

What Craig next said to him I wasn't able to hear, but I saw Sandy solemnly and emphatically shake his head, saying, "We'll beat him today," and I gathered from his words that he had been added to the vigilance committee.

Old man Nelson was busy with his own team. Mr. Craig went up to greet him next.

"How is it, Nelson?" he asked.

It was a very grave voice that answered him, "I hardly know, sir. But I am not through with the thing yet, though it seems there is little to hold to. What you said last night may be true enough, but it still doesn't give a man much to grab."

"All you want for a grip is what your hand can cover. What else would you have? And besides, do you know why you are still hanging on to your resolve of last night?"

The old man waited, looking at the minister seriously.

"Because He hasn't let go His grip of you."

"How do you know He's gripped me?"

"Now, look here, Nelson, what do you want—to quit this thing and give it all up?"

"No, no! For Heaven's sake! Why, do you think I have lost it?"

"Well, he's keener about being friends with you than you are! He's not about to let go of you! And I bet you haven't even stopped to thank Him."

The old man gazed at the minister, a light growing in his eyes.

"You're right. Thank God, you're right."

He turned quickly away, and went into the stable behind his team. It was a minute before he came out. Over his face was a light, and his eyes sparkled in joy.

"Can I do anything for you today?" he asked.

"Indeed you can," said the minister, taking his hand and shaking it very warmly. "Slavin has his program, and we have ours. It's a battle, Mr. Nelson," he said, "and we have to win it. We have to help the boys fight against the drink! I'm especially concerned about Sandy. He'll be all right till after his race. Then comes his time of danger."

"I'll stay with him," said old Nelson, in the tone of a man making a solemn vow, and immediately set off for the coffee tent.

"Here comes another recruit for your cause," I said walking up to the minister and pointing to Leslie Graeme, who was coming down the street at that moment in his small light sleigh.

"I'm not so sure. Do you think you could enlist him?"

I laughed. "You make me your co-conspirator?"

"Well," he replied, "isn't this now your fight too?"

"You make me think so! Well, all right, I'll see what I can do about my old friend Leslie."

I approached Graeme.

"What are you still doing here?" he asked in surprise. "I thought I had given you my final farewell last night."

"Plans changed," I replied. "Rather abruptly."

Then I went on to describe our hopes for the day, growing more and more enthusiastic as I spoke, while he sat listening in his sleigh with a quizzical smile I didn't quite like.

"He's got you already," he said. "I had a suspicion this might happen."

"Perhaps so," I laughed.

Just then the minister came up and greeted Graeme.

"What is my assignment, Mr. Craig?" he said, "for I know that this man"—here he nodded in my direction—"is simply your agent."

"Well," answered Craig, "I thought perhaps you would not mind presiding at dinner—I want it to go off well."

"That's all right," said Graeme, with an air of relief, "I expected something hard."

"It's good of you to agree," Craig replied as he turned away. "You are just in time for a cup of coffee, Mr. Graeme. But I must now go and see Mrs. Mavor."

"Who is Mrs. Mavor?" I asked again, this time of my friend.

"Why, she's the miners' guardian angel," he replied.

We put up the horses and set off for coffee at the tent.

4.
CHRISTMAS DAY RACE

The great event of the day was to be the four-horse race. Three teams were entered—one from the mines driven by Nixon, Craig's friend, a town citizens' team, and Sandy's from the lumber camp.

The race was really between the miners' team and that from the woods, for the citizens' team, though made up of speedy horses, had not been driven much together and were not well acquainted with either their driver or each other. The miners' team was made up of four bays, very powerful, a trifle heavy perhaps, but well-matched, perfectly trained, and perfectly handled by their driver. Sandy had his long rangy roans, and for leaders a pair of half-broken pinto broncos. The pintos, caught the summer before upon the Alberta prairies, were fleet as deer, but wicked and uncertain. They were Baptiste's special care and pride. If they would only run straight there was little doubt they would carry the roans and themselves to glory. But one could not tell the moment they might bolt or start kicking things to pieces.

Being the only non-partisan in the crowd I was asked to referee.

The race was about half a mile out and return, the first and last quarters being upon the ice. The course, after leaving the ice, led up from the river by a long easy slope to the level above, and at the further end curved somewhat sharply around the Old Fort.

The only rule attached to the race was that the teams should start from the scratch, make the turn of the Fort, and finish at the scratch. There were no annoying regulations about fouls. The man making the foul would find it necessary to reckon with the crowd, which was considered sufficient guarantee for a fair and square race. Owing to the hazards of the course, the result would depend upon the skill of the drivers quite as much as upon the speed of the teams. The points of hazard were at the turn round the Old Fort, and at a little ravine which led down to the river, where the road passed over a narrow long bridge made of logs.

From a point on the high bank of the river the whole course lay in open view. It was a scene full of life and vividly picturesque. There were miners in dark clothes and peak caps, citizens in ordinary garb, ranchmen in wide cowboy hats and buckskin shirts and leggings, some with gunbelts and pistols, a few half-breeds and Indians in native dress, and scattering through the crowd the lumbermen with gay red and blue plaid coats. It was a very good natured but extremely uncertain crowd. At the head of each horse stood a man, but at the pintos' heads Baptiste stood alone, trying to keep them calm, for they had been thrown into a frenzy of fear by the yelling of the crowd.

Gradually all became quiet. Then in the midst of the absolute stillness came the words, "Are you ready?" Then the pistol shot...and the great race had begun! Above the roar of the crowd came the shrill cry of Baptiste, as he struck his bronco with the palm of his hand, and swung himself into the sleigh beside Sandy as it shot past.

Like a flash the broncos sprang to the front, two lengths in front of the other teams. But, terrified by the yelling of the crowd, instead of bending to the left bank up which the road wound, they wheeled to the right and were almost across the river before Sandy could swing them back onto the course.

Baptiste's cries, a curious mixture of French and English, continued to strike through all other sounds till his sleigh gained the top of the slope to find the others almost a hundred yards in front, the citizens' team leading, with the miners' close behind.

The moment the pintos caught sight of the teams ahead of them, they set off at a terrific pace and steadily ate up the intervening space. Nearer and nearer the turn came, the eight horses in front, running straight and well within their speed. Behind them flew the pintos, running savagely with ears set back, leading well the big roans, thundering along and gaining at every bound.

Soon the citizens' team had almost reached the Fort, running hard and gradually pulling away from the miners' bays. But Nixon knew what he was about, and was simply steadying his team for the turn. The moment the Fort was reached, his wisdom showed itself, for in the turn the lead sleigh left the track, lost a moment or two in the deep snow, and before they could get back onto the road, the bays had swept superbly past.

On came the pintos, swiftly nearing the Fort. At the pace they were rushing forward, it appeared impossible they could make the turn. But Sandy knew his leading horses; they had their eyes on the two teams in front and needed no touch of rein. Without the slightest change in speed, the nimble-footed broncos rounded the turn, hauling the big roans and sleigh behind them, and within moments were falling in behind the citizens' team as both steadily began to regain their lost ground on the leaders.

The moment the turn was made, the next struggle was for the small bridge over the ravine. The bays in front, running with mouths wide open, were doing their best. Behind them, gaining every moment but running at the limit of their speed, came the lighter and fleeter citizens' team. And opposite them—now nearly even—the pintos were pulling hard, eager and fresh. Their temper was too uncertain to send them to the front. They ran well following, but when leading were not to be trusted. Besides, a bronco hates a bridge. So Sandy held them where they were, waiting and hoping for his chance after they were across the ravine.

Inch by inch the citizens' team crept up to the flank of Nixon's bays, with the pintos in turn hugging them closely. It looked as if all three would reach the bridge at the same moment. One would be destroyed at the very least, for the bridge was not a wide one. Sandy saw the danger but dared not check the pace of his leaders for fear of losing the race.

Suddenly, within but a few yards of the bridge, Baptiste threw himself upon the lines of rein, wrenched them out of Sandy's hands, and, with a quick swing, urged the pintos down the steep side of the ravine, instead of across the bridge, which was almost sheer ice with a thin coat of snow. It was a daring course to take, for the ravine, though not deep, was full of undergrowth, and was partially closed up by a brush heap at the further end.

With a yell Baptiste hurled his four horses down the slope and into the undergrowth. "Allons, mes enfants!" he cried. "Courage! Vite! Vite!"

Nobly they responded. Regardless of bushes and brush heaps, they tore their way through. But as they emerged, the hind bob-sleigh was hurled high in the air. Baptiste's cries rang out high and shrill, encouraging his team, not stopping till, with a plunge and a scramble, they cleared the brush heap lying at the mouth of the ravine and were out on the ice on the river, with Baptiste standing on the front bob, the box trailing behind, and Sandy nowhere to be seen.

Three hundred yards of the course remained.

The bays, perfectly handled, reached the bridge first, and in the descent to the ice were now leading the citizens' team by six sleigh lengths. Behind both came Baptiste.

51

It was now or never for the pintos. The rattle of the trailing box, together with the wild yelling of the crowd rushing down to the bank to watch, excited them to near madness, and, taking the bits in their teeth, they at last were let loose to do their first free running of the day. Past the citizens' team they dashed like a whirlwind, in no time making up the intervening space and were on the flanks of the miners' bays.

Nixon leaned over his team, yelling encouragement, and for the first time plying the hissing lash. Only fifty yards more. As with one voice the miners were yelling at the top of their lungs.

But Baptiste, waving his reins high in one hand, seized his whip with the other, whirled it about his head, and flung it with a fiercer shout then ever at the broncos. Like the bursting of a hurricane the pintos lept forward, still faster, pulled even to Nixon's team, and with a splendid final rush crossed the line, winners by less than their own length.

The shantymen had torn off their coats and were waving them wildly and tossing them high, while the ranchers added to the uproar by emptying their revolvers into the air in a way that could hardly help but make one nervous.

A wild quarter of an hour followed!

When the crowd was somewhat quieted, Sandy's forlorn figure appeared, walking slowly toward them. A dozen lumbermen ran to him, eagerly asking if he were hurt. But Sandy only shook his head, and cursed the little Frenchman for his foolhardy maneuver which cost them the race.

"Lost the race!" cried one of his friends, "Why, man, we've won it!"

Sandy's anger vanished in an instant, and he allowed himself to be carried on the shoulders of his admirers.

"Where is the lad?" was his first question.

"The broncos are off with him. He's likely down at the rapids by now."

"Let me go," shouted Sandy, setting off at a run following the track of the sleigh.

He had not gone far before he met Baptiste coming back with his team, quieted somewhat but foaming steadily. The roans were walking, but the two broncos were dancing and appeared eager to be at it again.

"Viola! Tank the bon Dieu, Sandy. You not keel, heh?" Ah! You one grand chevalier!" exclaimed Baptiste, hauling Sandy in and thrusting the reins back into his hands.

And so back they came, the sleigh box still dragging behind, the pintos executing figures on their hind legs, and Sandy holding them down. Only when Baptiste got them by the heads could they be induced to stand long enough to allow Sandy to be proclaimed winner of the race. Several of the lumbermen sprang up to the sleigh box with Sandy and Baptiste, among them Keefe, followed by Nelson, and the first part of the great day was over.

Slavin could not understand the new order of things. That a great event like the four-horse race should not be followed by "drinks all around" was to him incomprehensible. He disappeared into the crowd, but by no means was ready to concede defeat. He still had plenty of men with him.

Mr. Craig came up to me, looking anxiously toward Sandy in his sleigh.

"Poor Sandy," he said, "with emotions at such a high pitch, I fear he will be easily caught. Keefe has the devil's cunning."

"I'm sure he won't touch Slavin's whisky today," I said confidently.

"There'll be twenty bottles waiting to toast him in the stable," he replied. "He won't even need to go near the saloon. And we can't go following him about every step."

Then he stopped, apparently thinking what tack to take next.

5.
THE CHRISTMAS SERVICE

The sports were over.

There remained still an hour to be filled in before dinner. It was an hour full of danger to Craig's hope of victory, for the men were wild with excitement, ready for the most reckless means of slinging their dust, and restlessly idle besides—a disastrous combination.

I could not but admire the skill with which Jim Craig caught their attention.

"Gentlemen," he called out, "we've forgotten the judge of the great race. Three cheers for Mr. Connor!"

Two of the shantymen picked me up and hoisted me upon their shoulders, while the cheers were given.

"Announce the next Punch-and-Judy performance," he said to me in a low voice. I did so, giving a little speech, and was forthwith borne aloft through the street to the booth, followed by the whole crowd, still cheering.

The excitement of the crowd was contagious and caught me up. For the next hour I squeaked and worked the wires of the immortal and unhappy family in a manner I had never approached before. I was glad when Graeme poked his head in the back door to tell me to send the men in to dinner. This Mr. Punch did, and again with cheers for Punch's master they trooped tumultuously into the tent.

We had only well begun when Baptiste came in quietly but hurriedly and whispered to me—

"M'sieu Craig, he's gone to Slavin's and would lak you and M'sieu Graeme to follow queek. Sandy he's take on leet-le drink up at de stable, and he's go mad lak one devil."

I sent him for Graeme, who was presiding at dinner, and set off for Slavin's saloon at a run. There I found Mr. Craig and Nelson holding Sandy, more than half drunk, back from Slavin, who, stripped to his shirt, was coolly wait-ing with a taunting smile.

"Let me go, Craig!" Sandy was saying. "I am a good Presbyterian. He's a thief and he has my money, and I will beat it out of the soul of him!"

"Let him go, preacher," sneered Slavin. "I'll cool him off!"

"Let him go!" Keefe was shouting.

"Hand off!" Blaney echoed.

I pushed my way in. "What's up?" I said.

"Mr. Connor," said Sandy solemnly. "You are a gentle-man, and I am a good Presbyterian, and I can give you the Commandments and Reasons annexed to them. But he's a thief, and I am justified in getting my money out of his soul."

"But you won't get it in this way," I argued.

"He had my money!"

"He is a blank liar, and he's afraid to take it up," said Slavin in a low, contemptuous tone.

With a roar Sandy broke away and rushed at him. But without moving from where he stood, Slavin met him with a straight left-hander and laid him flat.

Sandy rose slowly, gazing around stupidly.

"He don't even know what hit him," laughed Keefe.

This roused the Highlander, and saying, "I'll settle you

later, Mister Keefe," he rushed in again at Slavin. Again Slavin met him with his left, staggering him, but before he fell Slavin took a step forward and delivered a terrific right hand blow straight on his jaw. Sandy fell down in a heap on the floor, amid the yells of Blaney, Keefe, and some others of the gang, just as Graeme and Baptiste walked in.

One look at Sandy lying senseless and Baptiste tore off his coat and hat, slammed them on the floor, and with a shriek rushed at Slavin. But Graeme caught him by the back of the neck.

"Hold on, little man," he said.

Then he turned to Slavin, pointed to Sandy who was gradually coming to himself under Nelson's care, and said, "What's this for?"

"Ask him," replied Slavin insolently.

"What's it all about, Nelson?"

Nelson explained that after drinking some at the stable after the race, followed by a glass at the Black Rock Hotel, Sandy had come down here with Keefe and the others, had lost his money, and was accusing Slavin of robbing him.

"Did you give him liquor?" questioned Graeme sternly.

"It's none of your business," replied Slavin, swearing at him.

"I shall make it my business. It's not the first time my men have lost money in this saloon."

"You lie," said Slavin.

"Slavin," returned Graeme quietly, "it is a pity you said that. Because unless you apologize, I will make you very sorry for your words."

"Apologize!" roared Slavin. "Apologize to you?" he added, calling him a vile name.

Graeme's face grew white. Then he spoke again. "Now you'll have to take it; no apology will do."

Slowly he stripped off his coat and vest. Mr. Craig stepped up and interposed, begging Graeme to let the matter pass.

56

"Surely he is not worth it," implored the minister.

"Mr. Craig," said Graeme with an easy smile, "you don't understand. No man can call me that name, and then procede to walk around afterward without answering for it."

Then turning to Slavin, he went on, "Now, if you want a minute's rest, I can wait."

Slavin's only answer was a curse.

"Blaney," said Graeme sharply, "you get back out of the way."

Blaney promptly stepped back to Keefe's side.

"Nelson," said Graeme, "you and Baptiste can see that they stay there."

The old man nodded and looked at Craig, who simply said, "Do the best you can."

It was a good fight which followed. Slavin had plenty of pluck, and for a time forced the match, Graeme guarding easily and jabbing him aggravatingly about the nose and eyes, drawing blood but not disabling him. Gradually a look of fear began to come into Slavin's eyes—something with which he was all too unfamiliar—and the beads of sweat began to show on his face. For the first time he appeared to have met his match.

"Are you sorry for your words yet, Slavin?" called out Graeme.

"Well, I am about to show you what you are made of."

He made one or two lightning passes, struck Slavin one, two, three terrific blows, and laid him quite flat and unconscious on the floor. Keefe and Blaney both sprang forward, but there was a savage kind of growl.

"Hold on there!"

It was old man Nelson looking at them along the barrel of his pistol. "You know me well enough, Keefe," he said. "You'll murder no one this time."

Keefe turned a shade of green and yellow, and fell back,

while Slavin slowly rose to his feet.

"Do you want any more?" said Graeme. "It's not much you could give by this time, but mind I have stopped playing with you. Put away your gun, Nelson. No one will interfere now."

Slavin hesitated, then rushed forward in dumb fury. Graeme stepped up to meet him, and we saw Slavin's heels in the air as he fell back upon his neck and shoulders, laying still.

"Bon!" yelled Baptiste. "Dat's bon stuff. Dat's larn him one good lesson." But immediately, almost in the same breath, he shrieked out a warning.

He was too late, however. There was a crash of breaking glass and Graeme fell to the floor with a long deep cut on the side of his head. Keefe had hurled a bottle with perfect aim, and then fled.

My first thought was that my friend was dead. Blood was flowing from the cut and he lay insensible. But as we carried him out, in a few seconds he began to groan and opened his eyes for a moment. Then he sank again into unconsciousness.

We'll take him to Mrs. Mavor's," said Craig. "It's nearest. Can you manage him?" he said to Baptiste, Nelson, and myself. "I'll run on to tell her."

She met us at the door. The moment I saw her I forgot our urgent business and stood simply looking.

"Come in! Come!" she said. "Bring him right in." Her voice was sweet and soft and firm.

We entered, following her, and laid him in a large room at the back of the shop over which Mrs. Mavor lived. Together we dressed the wound, her firm white fingers skillful as if with long training. Before the dressing was finished Craig left us. The time had come for the slide show in the church, and it was a critical moment in our fight to keep the men's attention held beyond the dinner hour.

"He's coming to," I said. "Go ahead, we can manage."

In a few moments more Graeme revived completely. Gazing about, he asked, "What's going on?" then, recollecting, he added, "Now I remember, that brute Keefe." He looked at me.

"Sorry to cause you all this trouble, old fellow," he said.

"Nonsense," I answered. "Mrs. Mavor and I have you in good control. The only thing you have to do is keep perfectly still."

"Mrs. Mavor!" he said in surprise.

She came forward, with a slight flush on her face.

"I think you know me, Mr. Graeme."

"I have often seen you about, and wished to know you. I am sorry to bring this trouble upon you."

"Not a word more about that," she replied. "Let me do all I can for you. And now the doctor says you are to lie still."

"The doctor...you mean Connor?" He chuckled lightly. "He is hardly there yet! But you don't know each other. Permit me to present Mr. Connor, Mrs. Mavor."

As she bowed slightly, her eyes looked into mine with a serious gaze, not inquiring exactly, yet searching my soul. As I looked into her eyes I forgot everything about me, and when I came to myself it seemed as if I had been away in some far place. It was not their color or their brightness. I can't even remember their color, and I have often looked into them. And they were not particularly bright. But they were clear, and one could look far down into them, and in their depths see a glowing, steady light. As I went to get some drugs from the Black Rock doctor, I found myself wondering about that far-down light, and about her voice, how it could get that sound from far away.

I found the doctor quite drunk, as indeed Mr. Craig had warned. But his medications were good, and I got what I wanted and quickly returned.

While Graeme slept Mrs. Mavor made me tea. As the

evening wore on I told her about the events of the day, dwelling with what was by this time nothing short of admiration upon Craig's generalship. She smiled.

"He got me too," she said. "Nixon was sent to me just before the sports, and I don't think he will break down today. I am so thankful!" Her eyes glowed.

After a long pause, she went on. "I promised Mr. Craig I would sing tonight." She hesitated a moment, then went on. "But it has been two years since I have been able to sing— two years," she repeated, "since"—and then her voice trembled—"since my husband was killed."

"I understand," I said, having no other word on my tongue, but in truth understanding hardly at all.

"And," she went on quietly, "I fear I have been selfish. It is hard to sing the same songs. We were very happy. But the miners like to hear me sing, and I think perhaps it helps them to feel less lonely, and keeps them from evil. I shall try tonight, if I am needed. Mr. Craig will not ask me unless he must."

Having fallen under her spell, I must confess to an anger at Craig as a result of her words. I would have seen every miner and lumberman in the place drunk before I would have asked her to sing one song while her heart ached so.

"He thinks only of those wretched miners and shantymen of his!" I said, none too kindly I fear.

She looked at me with curiosity in her eyes, and said gently, "And are they not Christ's too?"

This time I found no word to reply.

It was by now nearing ten o'clock, and I was wondering how the battle was going. I hoped that Mrs. Mavor would not be needed. But just then the door opened and old man Nelson and Sandy came in, the latter much battered and ashamed. They had been sent by Craig to bring Mrs. Mavor.

"I will come," she said simply. She saw me preparing to accompany her.

"Do you think you can leave him?" she asked.

"He will do fine under Nelson's care."

"Then I am glad, for I must take my little one with me. I did not put her to bed in case I should need to go, and I wouldn't think of leaving her alone."

When the three of us arrived several minutes later, we entered the church by the back door. I saw at once that even yet—as late as it was and as successful as Craig's plans had been thus far—the battle might easily still be lost.

Some miners had just come from Slavin's, evidently bent on breaking up the meeting. Slavin had apparently encited them to revenge for the collapse of the dance, which no one was able to enjoy with only a handful present. Craig was gallantly holding his ground, finding it hard work to keep the men in good humor and prevent a fight, for there was much agitation, and a number of the miners were more than half drunk.

The look of relief that came over his face when Craig caught sight of us told how anxious he had been. "Thank God," he said. "I was about to despair."

He immediately walked to the front and said in a loud voice—

"Gentlemen, if you wish it, Mrs. Mavor has come to sing."

There was dead silence. Someone began to applaud, but then Shaw, the foreman at the mines, stood up in the audience and said—

"You all know that three years ago I was known as 'Old Ricketts,' and that I owe all I am tonight, under God, to Mrs. Mavor, and"—and with a little quiver in his voice—"her baby. And we all know that for two years she has not sung, and we all know why. And what I say is, that if she does not feel like singing tonight, she should not have to go through pain herself just to keep a few drunken brutes of Slavin's crowd quiet. If we can't keep control of ourselves, she shouldn't have to do it for us."

There were deep growls of approval all over the church. Mr. Craig went to Mrs. Mavor, and after a word with her came back and said—

"Mrs. Mavor wishes me to thank her dear friend Mr. Shaw, but says she would like to sing."

Mr. Craig sat down to the organ and played the opening bars of the melody, *Oft in the Stilly Night*. Mrs. Mavor came to the front. With an exquisitely sweet smile upon a face that had clearly known sadness, she looked straight at us with her glorious eyes, and began to sing.

Her rich soprano voice rose and fell; now soft, now strong, but always filling the building, pouring around us floods of music. At the end of the first verse the few women in the church and some of the men had tears in their eyes. But when she began the words—

> *"When I remember all*
> *The friends once linked together,"*

sobs began to come on every side from the tender-hearted fellows for whom the song brought sad memories of far away homes. But she sang steadily on, the tone clearer and sweeter and fuller at every note. And when the sound of her voice died away, she stood looking at the men as if in wonder that they should weep.

No one moved. Mr. Craig played softly on. Wandering through many variations, he arrived at last at *Jesus, Lover of My Soul*.

As Mrs. Mavor sang the appealing words, her face was lifted up and she saw none of us. But she must have seen someone, for the cry in her voice could only have come from one who could see and feel help close at hand. On and on went the glorious voice, searching my soul's depths.

When she came to the words—

> *"Thou, O Christ, art all I want,"*

she stretched up her arms. By then she had quite forgotten

us. Her voice had taken her to other worlds, and she sang with such a fervor of abandon that my soul was ready to surrender anything. Judging from the response throughout the small church, I was not alone in my feeling.

The audience sat as in a trance. The grimy faces of the miners, for they never get quite white, were furrowed with the tracks of tears. Shaw by this time had his face lifted high, and I could tell he was seeing the stately halls of heaven. Nixon too had his vision—but what he saw was the face of the singer, with the shining eyes, and by the look of him, that was vision enough.

Immediately after her last note, Mrs. Mavor stretched out her hands to her little girl, who was sitting on my knee, caught her up, and walked quickly behind the curtain. Not a sound followed the singing: no one moved till she had disappeared. Then Mr. Craig came to the front, and, motioning me to follow Mrs. Mavor, began in a low, distinct voice—

"Gentlemen, it was not easy for Mrs. Mavor to sing for us tonight, and you all know she sang because she is a miner's wife, and her heart is still with the miners. But she sang, too, because her heart is His who came to earth this very day so many years ago to save us all. And she would make you all love Him too if she could. That is why she sang. For in loving Him you are saved from all base loves, and you know what I mean.

"So before we say good night, men, I would like to know if this is not a good time when all of you who mean to be better than you are should join together. Let us put from us this thing that has brought sorrow and shame to us and to those we love? What better time than on Christmas Day to pledge ourselves to fight the evils of drink? Some of you are strong; will you stand by and see your weaker friends and brothers robbed of the money they save for those far away, and robbed of the manhood that no money can buy or restore?

"Will the strong among you help? Why cannot we all

join hands? In this town we have too often seen the hell caused by drunkenness. Yet just a moment ago we were all looking into heaven. O men!" and his voice rang in beseeching agony through the building—"O men! Which shall be ours? For heaven's sake, let us help one another! Who will join me?"

I was looking out through a slit in the curtain. The men, already worked up to intense feeling by the music, were listening with set faces and gleaming eyes. As Craig made his appeal, he raised his hand high above him where he stood. Almost instantly Shaw, Nixon, and a hundred men sprang to their feet and held up their hands with him.

I have witnessed some thrilling scenes in my life, but never anything to equal that: the one man on the platform standing at full height, with a hundred men below standing straight, with arms up, almost motionless.

For a moment Craig kept them so, then again his voice rang out, even louder than before:

"All who mean it, say, 'By God's help, I will.' "

And immediately back from a hundred mouths came deep and strong the words, "By God's help, I will."

At this point Mrs. Mavor, whom I had quite forgotten, put her hand on my arm. "Go and tell them," she said, "I want them to come on Thursday night, next week, as they used to in the old days—go—quick."

I went and gave Craig her message. He held up his hand for silence.

"Mrs. Mavor wishes me to say that she will be glad to see you all, as in the old days, a week from Thursday evening. And I can think of no better place to give formal expression to our pledge of tonight."

There was a shout of acceptance. Then, at someone's call, the long pent-up feelings of the crowd found vent in three mighty cheers for Mrs. Mavor.

"Now for our old favorite hymn," called out Mr. Craig, "and Mrs. Mavor will lead us."

64

He sat down at the organ, played a few bars of "The Sweet By and By," and then Mrs. Mavor began. But not a single person joined in until she reached the refrain, and then they sang as only men with their hearts on fire can sing. But after the last verse Mr. Craig made a sign to Mrs. Mavor, and she sang alone, slowly and softly, and with eyes looking far away—

> *"In the sweet by and by,*
> *We shall meet on that beautiful shore."*

There was no further benediction. There seemed no need of one, and the men went quietly out. But over and over again the voice kept singing in my ears and in my heart, "We shall meet on that beautiful shore." And after the sleigh-loads of men had gone and left the street empty, as I stood with Craig in the moonlight that made the great mountains about seem very near us, from Sandy's sleigh we heard in the distance Baptiste's French-English voice. But the sound that floated down with the sound of the bells from the miner's sleigh was—

> *"We shall meet on that beautiful shore."*

"Well," I said at last. "It appears you have won your fight."

"*We* have won the fight," he replied. "For the moment at least."

Then, taking off his cap and looking up beyond the mountain-tops and the silent stars, he added softly, "Our fight, but His victory."

And thinking it all over, I could not say but perhaps he was right.

6.
MRS. MAVOR'S STORY

The days that followed the Black Rock Christmas were anxious and weary, but I would never change them for any other days of my life. For as after the burning heat or rocking storm the dying day lies beautiful in the tender glow of the evening, so these days have lost their weariness and now lie bathed in a misty glory in my memory. The years that bring us many ills, and that pass so stormfully over us, bear away with them the ugliness, the weariness, the pain that are theirs. But the beauty, the sweetness, the rest they leave untouched, for these are eternal. As the mountains that near at hand stand jagged and scarred, in the far distance repose in their soft robes of purple haze, so the rough present fades into the past, soft and sweet and beautiful.

My friend Leslie Graeme had been seriously wounded by the glass of the bottle thrown against his head. For many days and nights we waited in fear for the turn of the fever that came upon him, tending him hour by hour. But as I recall the time I can think only of the patience and gentleness and courage of her who stood beside me, bearing more than half my burden. And while I can see the face of Leslie

Graeme, white or flushed red, and hear his low moaning, I think chiefly of the bright face bending over him, and of the cool, firm, swift-moving hands that soothed and smoothed and rested, and the voice, like the soft song of a bird in the twilight, that never failed to bring peace.

Mrs. Mavor and I were together a great deal during those days. I made my home in Mr. Craig's cabin, but most of my time was spent beside my friend. We did not see much of Craig, for he was heart-deep with the miners, laying plans for the making of the League the following Thursday. And though he shared our anxiety and was ever ready to relieve us, his thoughts and his talk had mostly to do with the League.

Mrs. Mavor's evenings were given to the miners, but her afternoons were devoted mostly to Graeme and me. That was when I saw another side of her character. We would sit in her little dining room, where the pictures on the walls, the quaint old silver, and bottles of curiously cut glass, all spoke of other and different days, and thence we would roam the world of literature and art. Keenly sensitive to all the good and beautiful in these, she had her favorites among the masters. Shakespeare and Tennyson and Burns she loved, but not Shelly, nor Byron nor even Wordsworth. Browning she did not know. When we talked of music, she, adoring Wagner, soared upon the wings of the mighty Tannhauser, far above, into regions unknown, leaving me to walk soberly with Beethoven and Mendelssohn. Yet with all our free and honest talk, there was all the while that in her gentle courtesy which kept me from venturing into any chamber of her life whose door she did not set freely open to me. So I continued to find myself puzzled by her, and when Mr. Craig returned the next week from the Landing where he had been for several days, my first question was—

"Who is Mrs. Mavor? And how in the name of all that is gentle and pure and unlikely does she come to be here? And why does she stay?"

67

He would not answer me then. Whether it was that his mind was full of other things, or that he shrank from the tale, I do not know. But that night, when we sat down together beside his fire, he told me the story. He was worn with his long, hard drive, and with the burden of his work, but as he went on with his account, looking into the fire as he told it, he forgot all his present weariness and lived again the scenes he painted for me.

This was his story:

"I remember well my first sight of her," he began, "as she sprang from the front seat of the stagecoach to the ground, hardly touching her husband's offered hand. She looked to be a mere girl. Let's see—five years ago—she couldn't have been a day over twenty-three. She looked barely twenty. Her swift glance swept over the group of miners at the hotel door, and then rested on the mountains standing in all their autumn glory.

"I was proud of our mountains that evening. Turning to her husband, she exclaimed, 'O Lewis, aren't they grand!'

"Every miner lost his heart then and there, but all waited for Abe, the stage driver, to give his verdict before venturing an opinion. Abe said nothing until he had taken a preliminary drink. Then, calling all hands to fill up, he lifted his glass high, and said solemnly—

" 'Boys, here's to her.'

"Like a flash every glass was emptied, and Abe called out, 'Fill her up again, boys! Drinks are on me!'

"He was evidently quite worked up. Then he went on with solemn emphasis—

" 'Boys, you listen to me. She's a No. 1, the pure quill with a bead on it: she's a—,' and for the first time in his Black Rock history Abe was stuck for a word. Someone suggested 'angel.'

" 'Angel!' repeated Abe with contempt. 'Angel be blowed! Why angels ain't in the same month with her. I'd like to see any blanked angel swing my team around them curves without a shiver.'

" 'Held the lines herself, Abe?' asked a miner.

" 'That's what I say,' replied Abe, who then went off into a fusillade of scientific profanity, expressive of his esteem for the girl who had swung his team round the curves. And the miners nodded to each other, and winked their entire approval of Abe's performance, for this was his specialty.

"Very decent fellow, Abe, but his talk wouldn't print," said Craig.

Here he stopped, as if balancing Abe's virtues and vices.

"Well," I urged, "who *is* she?"

"Oh yes," he said, recalling himself, "she is an Edinburg young lady—met Lewis Mavor, a young Scotch-Englishman, in London—wealthy, good family, and all that, but fast, and going to pieces at home. His people, who own large shares in these Selkirk mines, as a last resort sent him out here to reform. Curiously innocent ideas those old country people have of the reforming properties of this Western atmosphere! They send their young bloods here to reform. Here! Here in this devil's campground, where a man's lust is his only law, and where, from sheer monotony most men eventually take themselves to the only excitement of the place—that offered by the saloon. Good people in the East hold up holy hands of horror at these godless miners. But I tell you, it's asking more than they're capable of to expect these boys to keep straight and clean in a place like this. I take my excitement from fighting the devil and doing my work. But these poor chaps—hard working, homeless, with no break or change in the routine—God help them and me!"

"Well," I persisted, "did Mavor reform?"

"Reform?" he repeated. "Not exactly. In six months he had broken through all restraint. And, mind you, it wasn't the other miners' fault—not a single miner helped him down the path he seemed determined to go. It was a sight to make angels weep when Mrs. Mavor would come to the saloon door every night for her husband. Every miner would vanish, for they could not look upon her shame, and they would send Mavor out in the charge of Billy Breen, a queer little chap who had belonged to the Mavors in some way in the old country. And between the two of them they would get him home. How she stood it puzzles me to this day. But she never made any sign of dismay, and her courage never failed. It was always a bright, brave, proud face she held up to the world—except in church. There it was different. I used to preach my sermons, I believe, mostly for her—but never so that she could suspect—as cheerily as I could. And as she listened, and especially as she sang—how she used to sing in those days!—there was no touch of pride in her face, though the courage never died out, but silent appeal was written there. I could have cursed aloud the cause of her misery, or wept for the pity of it. Before her baby was born, her husband seemed to pull himself together for a time, for he was quite mad about her. And from the day the baby came—talk about miracles!—from that day he never drank a drop. She gave the baby over to him, and the baby simply absorbed him.

"He was a new man. He could not drink whisky and kiss his baby. And the miners—it was really absurd if it were not so pathetic. It was the first baby in Black Rock, and they used to crowd Mavor's shop and peep into the room at the back of it—I forgot to tell you that when he lost his position as manager in the mines from his drinking, he opened a small hardware shop—they would crowd in for a chance to be asked in to see the baby.

"I came upon Nixon one time standing at the back of the shop after he had seen the baby for the first time. And he was sobbing hard. To my question he replied, 'It's just like my own back home.'

70

"You can't understand this, Connor, but to men who have lived so long in the mountains that they have forgotten what a baby looks like, who have experienced humanity only in its roughest, foulest form for years, this little child, sweet and clean and innocent, was like an angel fresh from heaven, the one link in all that black camp that bound them to what was purest and best in their past.

"And to see the mother and her baby handle the miners!

"It was beautiful beyond words! I shall never forget the shock I got one night when I found 'Old Ricketts' holding and tending the baby. A drunken old beast he was. But there he sat, sober enough, making extraordinary faces at the baby, who was grabbing at his nose and whiskers and cooing in blissful delight. Poor old Ricketts looked as if he had been caught stealing, and muttered something about having to go, gazed wildly round for some place to lay the baby, when in came the mother, saying in her own sweet, frank way, 'Oh, Mr. Ricketts'—she didn't find out till afterward that his name was Shaw—'would you mind keeping her just a little longer? I shall be back in a few minutes.' And Ricketts mumbled something about guessing he could wait.

"But within six months mother and baby, between the two of them, transformed 'Old Ricketts' into Mr. Shaw, fire-boss of the mines. And then in the evenings, when she would be singing her baby to sleep, the little shop would be full of miners, listening in dead silence to the baby-songs, and the English songs, and the Scottish lullabies, all of which she poured forth without stint, for she sang more for them than for her baby.

"No wonder they adored her!

"She was so bright, so gay! She brought light with her when she went into the camp, into the mines' pits—for she went down to see the men work—or into a sick miner's shack. And many a man, lonely and sick for home or wife or baby or mother, found in that back room of the humble

71

hardware shop cheer and comfort and courage. And to many a poor broken wretch that room became, as one miner put it, 'the.parlor of heaven.' "

Craig paused. I waited. Then he went on slowly.

"For a year and a half that was the happiest home in all the world, till one day—"

He put his face in his hands and shuddered.

"I don't think I can ever forget the awful horror of that bright fall afternoon when Old Ricketts came breathless to me and gasped, 'Come, for the dear Lord's sake!' and I rushed out after him.

"At the mouth of the shaft lay three men dead. One was Lewis Mavor. After his reformation he had been hired back to superintend the running of a new shift. The other two men of his crew, half drunk with Slavin's whisky, had set off a shot of dynamite prematurely, to the destruction of all three. They were badly burned, but Mavor's face was untouched. A miner was sponging off his face. The others were standing about waiting for me to speak. But I could find no word. My heart was sick, thinking, as I knew all of them were, of the young mother and her baby waiting at home. So I stood for several moments, looking stupidly from one to the other, trying to find some reason—coward that I was— why another should bear the news rather than I.

"And then all at once as we stood there, looking at one another and upon the three dead men on the ground, there broke upon us the sound of a voice mounting high above the birch tops, singing the haunting Scottish memory of that land's beloved bonnie Prince Charlie. But as we heard her singing the words, we knew they contained a dreadful meaning she did not yet know—

> " 'Will ye no' come back again?
> Will ye no' come back again?
> Better lo'ed ye canna be,
> Will ye no' come back again?'

"A strange terror seized us. Instinctively the men closed up in front of the body and stood in silence. Nearer and nearer came the clear, sweet voice, ringing like a silver bell up the steep mountain as she came to meet her husband—

" 'Sweet the lav'rock's note and lang,
Liltin' wildly up the glen,
But aye tae me he sings ae sang,
Will ye no' come back again?'

"Before the verse was finished, Ricketts had dropped on his knees, sobbing out brokenly, 'O God! O God, have pity on her...have pity!'

"Every man took off his hat. And still the voice came nearer and nearer, singing so brightly the refrain,

" 'Will ye no' come back again?'

"It became unbearable. Suddenly old Ricketts, sprang to his feet, gripped me by the arm, and cried pitifully, 'Go to her, for heaven's sake, go to her!'

"I hardly remember what came next. Suddenly I found myself standing in her path and seeing her holding out her hands full of red lillies, saying, 'Aren't they lovely? Lewis is so fond of them!'

"With the promise of much finer ones, I turned her down a path toward the river, talking I know not what folly, till her great eyes grew grave, then anxious, and my tongue stammered and became silent. Then, laying her hand upon my arm, she said with gentle sweetness, 'Tell me your trouble, Mr. Craig,' and I knew my agony had come.

"I burst out, 'Oh, if only it *were* my trouble!'

"She turned white, and with her deep eyes—you've noticed her eyes—drawing the truth out of mine, she said, 'Is it mine, Mr. Craig, and my baby's?'

"I waited, thinking with what words to begin. She put one hand to her heart, and with the other caught a little poplar tree that shivered under her grasp, and said with white lips, but even more gently, 'Tell me.'

"I wondered how my voice could be so steady as I said, 'Mrs. Mavor, God will help you and your baby. There has been an accident—and it is all over.'

"She was a miner's wife, and there was no need for more. I could see the pattern of the sunlight falling through the trees upon the grass. I could hear the murmur of the river, and the cry of the catbird in the bushes, but we seemed to be in a strange unreal world. Suddenly she stretched out her hands to me, and with a little moan said, 'Take me to him.'

" 'Sit down for a moment or two,' I begged her.

" 'No, no, I am quite ready. See,' she added quietly, 'I am quite strong.'

"I set off by a shortcut leading to her home, hoping the men would be there before us. But she passed me, walking swiftly through the trees, and I followed in fear. As we came near the main path I heard the sound of feet, and I tried to stop her. But she too had heard, and knew.

" 'Please, let me go,' she said piteously, 'you need not fear.' And I had no more heart to try to stop her.

"In a little clearing among the pines we met the bearers. When the men saw her they laid down their burden gently upon the carpet of yellow pine needles. And then, for they had the hearts of true men in them, they went away into the forest and left her alone with her dead husband. She went swiftly to his side, making no cry, but kneeling beside him she stroked his face and hands, and touched his curls with her fingers, murmuring all the time soft words of love.

" 'O my darling, my bonnie, bonnie darling, speak to me! Will ye no' speak to me just one little word? O my love, my love, my heart's love! Listen, my darling!' And she put her lips to his ear, whispering, and then the awful stillness.

"Suddenly she lifted her head and scanned his face, and then, glancing round with a wild surprise in her eyes, she cried, 'He will not speak to me!'

"I signalled to the men, and as they came forward I went to her and took her hands.

" 'Oh,' she said, with a wail in her voice, 'he will not speak to me.!

"The men were sobbing aloud. She looked at them with wide-open eyes of wonder. 'Why are you weeping? Will he never speak to me again? Tell me,' she insisted gently. The words were running through my head—

" *'There's a land that is fairer than day.'*

and I said them over to her, holding her hands firmly in mine. She gazed at me as if in a dream. And the light slowly faded from her eyes as she said, tearing her hands from mine and waving them toward the mountains and the woods—

" 'But never more here? Never more here?'

"I believe in heaven and the other life," said Craig pensively, "but I confess that for a moment it all seemed shadowy beside the reality of this warm, bright world, full of life and love.

"She was very ill for two nights. And when the coffin was closed a new baby lay in the father's arms.

"She slowly came back to life. But there were no more songs. The miners still come about her shop, and talk to her baby, and bring her their sorrows and troubles. But though she is always gentle, almost tender with them, no man ever says, 'Sing.' And that is why I am so glad she sang last week. It will be good for her and good for them."

"Why does she stay?" I asked.

"Mavor's people wanted her to go back and live with them," he replied. "They have money—she told me about it. But her heart is in the grave up there under the pines. And besides, she hopes to do something for the miners, and she will not leave them."

"But with her face and manner, and her voice, she could be anything she liked in Edinburgh or London," I said. "She could have any stage she wanted."

"And why Edinburgh or London?" he asked coolly.

"Certainly they would be better than this!" I replied.

"Nazareth was good enough for the Lord of glory," he answered with a smile.

For a moment I was silent, then said: "How long will she stay?"

"Till her work is done, I suppose," he replied.

"And when will that be?" I asked.

"When God chooses," he answered seriously. "And don't you ever think but that it is worthwhile. The greatest value of a man's, or a woman's life work is not that crowds stare at it, or that people applaud it. Read history, man!"

He rose abruptly and began to walk about. "Don't miss the whole meaning of the Life that lies at the foundation of all religion. Eternal value is not measured in the way man sees! Yes," he added, almost to himself, "the work God gives us to do is worth doing—worth even her doing!"

I must admit that, even with as much as I had seen in my few days at Black Rock, I found it hard to agree with him then. I was still an observer in the spiritual things to which my eyes were gradually being opened.

But the spell of Craig, and Mrs. Mavor, was upon me, and the light of after years revealed to me that the words of the mountain minister proved him indeed wiser than I. A man, to see far, must climb to some height, and I was too much upon the plain in those days to catch even a glimpse of distant sunlit uplands of triumphant achievement that lie beyond the valley of self-sacrifice.

But without knowing it, I was being borne upward, toward mountains not so easily visible as those which surrounded the little mining village of Black Rock.

7.
THE MAKING OF THE LEAGUE

Thursday morning found Craig anxious, even gloomy, but with fight in every line of his face.

"I've tried for two years to get these men to wake up to their folly," he said, "and if it falls through now, I shall find it hard to bear."

"Why, surely their resolve will stick after that scene in the church," I said.

"Poor fellows," he replied. "Whisky is about the only excitement they have, and they find it pretty tough to give it up, no matter what they might say in a moment of enthusiasm in a church meeting. And a lot of the men are just plain against the total abstinence idea in the first place."

"Can't you succeed without going that far?"

"No, I fear not. Some of them talk of compromise, about moderate drinking. They say they will stop going to the saloon and drink quietly in their shacks. The moderate drinker may have his place in other countries, though I can hardly see it. I haven't thought that out, but here the only safe man is the man who quits it dead and fights it straight on. Anything else is not going to work. Because the first drink is always the most dangerous, and usually always leads to many more. These men just don't have the willpower to stop at one or two."

I had not gone in much for total abstinence myself. By no stretch of the imagination did I consider myself a strong drinker, but I enjoyed myself now and then. Yet my confidence in Craig was by now so strong that I listened attentively to him, thinking that possibly there was a side to the question which I had never considered. As to Black Rock, I could see that perhaps it did have to be one thing or the other.

We found Mrs. Mavor bright. She shared Mr. Craig's anxiety but not his gloom. Her mood was of a serenity that refused to believe in possible defeat and thus lifted the spirit. As evening after evening the miners dropped into the cozy room downstairs, with her talk and her songs she charmed them till they were wholly hers. She took for granted their loyalty, trusted them utterly, and so made it difficult for them to be other than true men.

By the time Thursday evening came, Mrs. Mavor's large storeroom, which had been fitted up with seats, was already crowded with miners when Craig and I entered.

After a glance over the crowd, Craig said, "There's the manager of the mines."

I saw a tall man, fair, whose chin fell away to the vanishing point, and whose hair was parted in the middle, talking to Mrs. Mavor. She was dressed in some soft rich stuff that became her well, looking as beautiful as ever. But there was something quite new in her manner. She looked the highbred lady, the hostess, whose gentle dignity and sweet grace, while winning, made familiarity impossible.

The manager was doing his best, and appeared well pleased with himself. "She'll get him if anyone can," Craig went on. "I have not had much luck with him."

I stood looking at the men, and a fine lot of fellows they were. Free, easy, bold in their bearing, they gave no sign of awkwardness, and from their frequent glances toward Mrs. Mavor, I could see they were always conscious of her presence. No men are so truly gentle in the presence of a good woman as are Westerners. They were of all classes and ranks originally, but now, and in this country of real measurements, they ranked simply according to the "man" in them.

"See the handsome young chap of dissipated appearance?" said Craig. "That's Vernon Winton, an Oxford graduate, blue blood, awfully plucky, but quite gone with the drink. When he gets repentant, instead of shooting himself, he comes to Mrs. Mavor. But it never sticks."

"From Oxford University to Black Rock mining camp is something of a step," I replied.

"The queer-looking chap in the corner is Billy Breen. How in the world has he got here?" went on Mr. Craig.

Odd looking he definitely was. A little man with a small head set on heavy square shoulders, long arms, and huge hands that sprawled all over his body; altogether a most ungainly specimen of humanity.

By this time Mrs. Mavor had finished with the manager and was in the center of a group of miners. Her grand old-country air was gone, and she was again their comrade, their friend, one of themselves. Nor did she assume the role of entertainer, but rather, with a half-shy air, she cast herself upon their chivalry, and they truly behaved like gentlemen to her.

It is hard to make any man talk, especially a Western man. And most difficult of all is to loosen the tongue of an old-timer. But this gift was hers, and it stirred my admiration to see her draw on a grizzled veteran to tell how, twenty years ago, he had crossed the Great Divide over the Rockies, and had seen and done what no longer fell to men to see or do in these *new* days of the 1880's.

And so she won the old-timer. But it was beautiful to see the innocent guile with which she caught her husband's old friend, Billy Breen, in an altogether different way, drawing him to her corner near the organ. What she was saying I didn't know, but poor Billy was protesting, waving his big hands.

In another minute the meeting came to order, with Shaw in the chair, and the handsome young Oxford man acting as secretary. Shaw stated the object of the meeting in a few halting words. But when he came to speak of the pleasure he and all the others felt in being together again in that room, his words flowed in a stream, warm and full.

Then there was a pause and Mr. Craig was called. But he knew better than to speak at that point. Finally Nixon rose haltingly. But as he caught a bright smile from Mrs. Mavor, he straightened himself as if for a fight.

"I ain't no good at makin' speeches," he began, "but it ain't speeches we want. We've got somethin' to do, and what we want to know is how to do it. And to be right plain, we want to know how to drive this cursed whisky out of Black Rock. You all know what it's doing for us—at least some of us. And it's high time to stop it now, or for some of us it'll mighty soon be too late. And the only way to stop its work is to quit drinkin' it and help others to quit. I hear some talk of a League—a pact. And what I say is, if it's a League out and out against whisky, a Total Abstinence right to the ground, then I'm with it. Lord knows it'll be uphill work, and tough going for me, too. But I know what's got to be done, so I'm for it. There—that's my talk—I move we make that kind of League together."

Nixon sat down amid cheers and a chorus of remarks, but he waited for the smile and the glance that came to him from the beautiful face in the corner, and with that he seemed content.

Again there was silence. Then the secretary rose with a slight flush on his handsome, delicate face, and seconded the motion. If they would pardon a personal reference he would give them his reasons, he said. He had come to this country to make his fortune, and now he was anxious to make enough to enable him to go home with some degree of honor. His home held everything that was dear to him. Between him and that home, between him and all that was good and beautiful and honorable, stood whisky, which took his money and all his resolve. "I am ashamed to confess," he said, and the flush deepened on his cheek, and his lips grew thinner, "that I feel the need of some such agreement between us, or I'm not sure I can make it on my own." His handsome face, his perfect style of address, but more than all his show of nerve—for these men knew how to value that—made a strong impression on his audience, although there were no following cheers. On Mrs. Mavor's face was a look of tender, wistful pity, for she knew how much the words had cost the lad.

Then up rose a sturdy, hard-featured man, with a burr in his voice that proclaimed his Scottish birth. His name was George Crawford, I learned afterward, but everyone called him Geordie. He was a character in his way, fond of his glass, but though he was never known to refuse a drink, he had never been known to be drunk. He took his drink, for the most part, with bread and cheese in his own shack, or with a friend or two in a sober, respectable way, but on no occasion could be induced to join the wild carousals in Slavin's saloon. He made the highest wages, but was far too true a Scot to spend his money recklessly. Everyone waited eagerly to hear Geordie's mind. He spoke solemnly, as befitted a Scotsman expressing a deliberate opinion, and carefully, as if choosing his best English, for when Geordie became excited no one in Black Rock could understand him.

"Maister Chairman," he said. "I'm aye for temperance in all things."

There was a round of laughter at his words.

"I'll no deny," Geordie went on in an explanatory tone, "that I tak a mornin', an' maybe a nip at noon, an' a wee drap after wark in the evenin', an' whiles a sip o' toddy wi' a friend the cauld nights. But I'm no guzzler, an' I dinna gang in wi' those loons flingin' aboot good money."

"And that's thrue for you, me bye," interrupted a rich Irish brogue, to the delight of the crowd. But Geordie went on calmly—

"An' I canna bide yon saloon where they sell such awful-like stuff—it's more like lye than good whiskey—an' where ye're never sure o' yer right change. It's an awful place!"—Geordie was beginning to warm up now—"Ye can just smell the sulpher when ye go in. But I dinna care too much aboot them Temperance Societies neither, wi' their pledges an' all their talk. An' I canna see what harm can come to a man by takin' a bottle o' good Glenlivet home wi' him. I canna bide teetotalin' more than I can Slavin's place."

Geordie's speech was followed by loud applause, partly appreciative of Geordie himself, but largely sympathetic with his position.

Two or three men followed in the same strain, advocating a league for mutual improvement and social purposes, but without the teetotal pledge. They were against the saloon, but didn't see why they should not take a drink now and then.

Finally the manager rose to support his "friend" *Mistah* Crawford, ridiculing the idea of a total abstinence pledge as fanatical and indeed absurd. He was opposed to the saloon and would like to see a club formed, with comfortable club room, books, magazines, pictures, games, anything to make the time pass pleasantly. But it was absurd to ask men to abstain from a few nourishing drinks because a few made beasts of themselves. He concluded by offering $50 toward the support of such a club.

It appeared that the current of feeling was setting strongly against the total abstinence idea, and Craig's face was growing harder, his eyes gleaming like coals.

Then the minister pulled off a bit of generalship. He

proposed that since they had two plans clearly before them, they should take a few minutes' intermission in which to make up their minds, and he was sure they would be glad to have Mrs. Mavor sing. In the interval the men talked in groups, eagerly, even fiercely arguing the merits of the two sides, yet hampered in the forceful expression of their opinions by the presence of Mrs. Mavor, who glided from group to group, dropping a word here and a smile there. She reminded me of a general riding along the ranks, bracing his men for the coming battle. She paused beside Geordie, spoke earnestly for a few moments while Geordie gazed solemnly at her. Then she came back to Billy in the corner near me. What she was saying I could not hear, but Billy was protesting again, spreading out his hands before him. Then she came to me.

"Poor Billy," she said. "He was good to my husband." She was speaking very softly. "And he has a good heart. But I can't be sure."

I moved over beside Billy, whose eyes were following Mrs. Mavor as she went to speak to Mr. Craig. "Well," I said, "you all seem to have a high opinion of her."

He gave me a quick glance out of his little, deep-set, dark-blue eyes, and began, slowly at first, to talk to me. Before he knew it, he had opened his heart. He told me, in his quaint speech, how again and again she had taken him in and cared for him in his drunkenness, and encouraged him, and sent him out with a new heart for his personal battle, until, for very shame's sake at his own weakness, he had kept out of her way for many months, going steadily down.

"Now, I ain't got no grip o' myself. But when she says to me tonight, says she, 'Oh, Billy'—she calls me Billy to myself" (this he said with a touch of pride)—" 'Oh, Billy,' she says, 'we must have a total abstinence league tonight, and I want you to help!' and she keeps a-lookin' at me with those eyes o' hern till, if you believe me, sir," lowering his voice to an emphatic whisper, "though I knowed I couldn't help none, afore I knowed it I had promised her I would. It's her eyes. When them eyes says 'do,' hup you steps and 'does'."

I remembered my first look into her eyes, and I could quite understand Billy's submission. Just as she began to sing I went over to Geordie and took my seat beside him.

She began with an English slumber song, "Sleep, Baby, Sleep," and then sang a love song. But not until she began the nostalgic Scots' "My Ain Fireside" did she truly begin to move the men. Geordie gave a sigh of satisfaction. And when she finished the first verse he gave me a dig in the ribs with his elbow that took my breath away, whispering to me, "Man, do ye hear that?" And again I found her spell had come upon me. It was not her voice, but the great soul behind it that thrilled and compelled. She was seeing, feeling, living what she sang, and her voice showed us her heart. The cozy fireside, with its bonnie, blithe blink, where no care could abide, but only peace and love, was vividly present to her, and as she sang we saw it too.

When she came to the last verse—

"When I draw in my stool
    On my cosy hearth-stane,
My heart loups sae licht
    I scarce ken't for my ain,"

there was a feeling of tears in the flowing song, and we knew the words had brought her a picture of the fireside that would always seem empty. I felt the tears in my eyes, and, wondering at myself, I cast a quick glance at the men about me. I saw that they too were looking through their hearts' windows upon firesides and ingleneuks that gleamed from afar.

Then she sang, "The Auld Hoose," and Geordie, giving me another poke said, "That's my ain sang."

When I asked him what he meant, he whispered fiercely,

"Quiet, man!" and I obeyed, for his face looked dangerous.

In a pause between the verses I heard Geordie saying to
himself, "Ay, I must give it up, I dinna doobt."

"What?" I ventured to ask.

"Man, but ye're an inquisitive one," after which I sub-
sided into silence.

Immediately after the meeting was again called to order,
Mr. Craig made his speech, and it was a fine bit of work.
Beginning with a clear statement of the object in view, he set
in contrast the two kinds of leagues proposed. One, a league
of men who would take whisky in moderation; the other, a
league of men who were pledged to drink nothing themselves, and to prevent in every honorable way others from
drinking. There was no long argument, but he spoke heated-
ly. And as he appealed to the men to think, each not of
himself alone, but of the others as well, the yearning, born
of his long months of desire and toil, vibrated in his voice
and reached to the heart. Many men looked uncomfortable
and uncertain, and even the manager began to look none too
cheerful.

At this critical moment, all at once Billy Breen shuffled
out to the front, and in a voice shaking with nervousness and
emotion, began to speak.

"I ain't no bloomin' temperance orator, and mayhap I
ain't got no right to speak here, but I gots somethin' to say
and I'm agoin' to say it.

"Parson," he went on, "he say it is whisky or no whisky
in this here club. If ye ask me, which ye don't, then no
whisky, says I. And if ye ask why?—well, just look at me!
Once I could mine more coal than any man in the camp, and
now I ain't fit to be a sorter. Once I had some pride and
ambition. Now I just waits around for someone to say,
'Here, Billy, do this or do that.' Once I made good pay and
sent it home regular to my poor old mother. But I ain't now
sent her none for a year and a half. Once Billy was a good

85

fellow and had plenty of friends. Now Slavin hisself kicks him out. And why? Because when Billy had money in his pocket, every man in this bloomin' camp says, 'Hello, Billy, what'll ye have?' And there's whisky at Slavin's and there's whisky in the shacks, and every holiday and every Sunday there's whisky. And when ye feel bad it's whisky, and when ye feel good it's whisky, and everywhere and always it's whisky, whisky, whisky! And now ye're goin' to stop it, and how? The manager, he says pictures and magazines. He takes his wine and his beer like a gentleman, he does, and he don't have no use for Billy Breen. But supposin' Billy wants to stop bein' such a beast and starts atryin' to be a man again, and when he gets good and dry, along comes someone and says, 'Hello, Billy, have a wee one with me,' it ain't pictures nor magazines that'd stop him then. Pictures and magazines! God help the man as ain't got nothin' but pictures and magazines to help when he's got a devil inside and a devil outside ashovin' and adrawin' him down to hell. And that's where I'm agoin' straight, and yer bloomin' League, whisky or no whisky, can't help me. But," and he lifted his trembling hands above his head, "if ye stop the whisky aflowin' round this camp, ye'll stop some of these lads that's afollowin' me hard. Yes, you and you and you!" and his voice rose to a wild pitch as he shook a trembling finger at one and another.

"Man, it's gruesome to hear him," said Geordie, "he's no steddy on his feet!" He reached out for Billy as he went stumbling past, pulling him down to a seat beside him, saying, "Sit doon, lad, sit doon. We'll make a man o' ye yet." Then he rose.

"Maister Chairman," he said, "I dinna doobt we'll jist hae to give it up."

"Give it up?" called out Nixon. "Give up the League?"

"Na, na, lad! Give up the wee drap o' whisky. It's no that good anyway, an' it's a terrible price. Man, if ye go to

Henderson's in Buchanan Street in Gleska, ye ken, ye'll get more for three-an'-sixpence than ye will at Slavin's for five dollars. An' Henderson's won't get ye mad like Slavin's, but goes doon smooth an' soft-like. But we canna get that here, an' so I'm thinkin' for mysel', I'll jist sign this teetotal thing."

And with the words, up he strode to the table and put his name down in the book Craig had ready. Then to Billy he said, "Come on, lad! Put yer name doon, an' we'll stand by ye."

Poor Billy looked around helplessly, his nerve all gone, and sat still. There was a swift rustle of garments, and in a moment Mrs. Mavor was beside him. In a voice that only Billy and I could hear, she said, "You'll sign with me, won't you, Billy?"

Billy gazed at her with a hopeless look in his eyes, and shook his little head. She leaned slightly toward him, smiled brightly, and, touching his arm gently, said—

"Come, Billy, there's no fear," and in a lower voice, "God will help you."

As Billy went up, following close behind Mrs. Mavor, a hush fell on the men until he had put his name to the pledge. Then they began to come up, man by man, and sign. Craig sat with his head down till I touched his shoulder. He took my hand and held it fast, and said simply, under his breath, "Thank God!"

And so the League was made.

8.
JIM CRAIG'S VISION

When I grow weary with the conventions of Christianity, and sick in my soul from feeding upon the husks that the churches often offer me in the shape of elaborate services and eloquent discourses, then I go back in my memory to those precious days in early 1883. The weariness and doubt leave me when I recall the spiritual communion in Black Rock, and I grow humble and strong. The simplicity and rugged grandeur of the faith, the humble gratitude of the rough men I see about the table, and the calm radiance of one saintly face, rest and reassure me.

Not even its most enthusiastic apologist would call Black Rock a religious community. But it possessed in a marked degree that eminent Christian virtue of tolerance. All creeds, all shades of religious opinion, were allowed, and it was generally conceded that the varying beliefs of one man were as good as another.

During the weeks following the making of the League, however, this open-minded attitude gradually gave way in the face of keen investigation and criticism. Mr. Craig was responsible for the former, which was of course a good and highly beneficial thing, for he set the men to study the life of Jesus and thus gain strength for their personal battles.

But if anyone more than another was to be blamed for the rise of intolerance which gradually grew in the village, that man was Geordie Crawford. He had his set beliefs from the Established Kirk of Scotland, and now that things "religious" had assumed greater import in the daily life of the community, he began to make his voice heard.

When Mr. Craig announced his intention of having the Sacrament of the Lord's Supper observed, Geordie produced his "expert opinion" on the matter, and many matters related. As no other man in the village was equipped with like spiritual credentials, Geordie constituted himself a kind of kirk-watchdog, charged with the double duty of guarding the entrance to the Lord's Table, and of keeping an eye upon the theological opinions of the community, and more particularly upon such members of it as gave evidence of possessing any opinions definite enough for statement.

It came to be Mr. Craig's habit to drop into the League-room, and toward the close of the evening to have a short Scripture lesson from the Gospels. Geordie's opportunity came after the meeting was over and Mr. Craig had left. The men would hang about and talk the lesson over, expressing opinions either favorable or unfavorable. All sorts of views, religious and otherwise, were aired. The originality of the ideas, the disregard for any particular creed or denomination, the honest frankness of the men, and the down-to-earth forcefulness of the language they used all combined to make these discussions marvelous indeed, perhaps like none other of their kind. The passage between Abe Baker, the stage driver, and Geordie was particularly rich. It followed upon a very telling lesson on the parable of the Pharisee and the Publican.

The chief actors in that wonderful story were transferred to the Black Rock stage, and were presented in miner's costume. Abe was particularly well pleased with the scoring of the "blanked old rooster who crowed so blanked high." Geordie's quiet remark "that it was no credit to a man to be a sinner" made him angry. And when Geordie went on to urge the importance of right conduct and respectability, Abe was led to pour forth vials of contemptuous wrath upon the hypocrites who thought themselves better than other people. But Geordie was quite unruffled, and lamented the ignorance of men who, brought up in "Epeescopawlyun or Methody" churches, could hardly be expected to detect the Antinomian or Arminian heresies.

"My mother was a Methodist!" countered Abe, boiling hot, "and I'll back any blanked Methodist against any blankety blank long-faced, lantern-jawed, skinflint Presbyterian!"

This charge he was eager to maintain to any man's satisfaction if he would kindly step outside.

Geordie was quite unmoved, but hastened to assure Abe that he meant no disrespect to his mother, who he had "no doobt was a clever enough woman, to judge by her son."

Abe was quickly appeased, and offered to set up the drinks all round. But Geordie, with evident reluctance, had to decline. "Na, na, lad," he said, "I'm a League man, ye ken," and I was sure that Geordie at that moment felt that membership in the League had its drawbacks.

Nor was Geordie too sure of Craig's orthodoxy. And though he was an absolute slave to Mrs. Mavor, he could not help lamenting her doctrinal condition—

"She's a fine woman, nae doobt, but poor creature, she's fair carried away wi' the errors o' them Epeescopawlyuns."

It fell to Geordie, therefore, as a sacred duty, in view of the laxity of those who seemed to be the pillars of the Church, to be all the more watchful and unyielding. But he was delightfully inconsistent when confronted with particulars. In conversation with him one night after a meeting, when he had been especially hard on the ignorant and godless, I innocently changed the subject to Billy Breen, whom

Geordie had taken to his shack since the night of the League. He was very proud of Billy's success in the fight against whisky, the credit for which he divided unevenly between Mrs. Mavor and himself.

"He's fair daft aboot her," he explained to me, "and I'll no deny that she's a great help, ay, a considerable assistance. But, man, she doesna ken the whisky an' the inside o' a man that's wantin' it. Ay poor lady, she does her part, an' when ye're a bit restless after yer day's work, it's like a walk in a bonnie glen on a summer eve, wi' the birds liltin' aboot, to sit in yon room and hear her sing. But when the night is on, and ye canna sleep, but wakens wi' an awful thirst and wi' dreams o' cosy firesides and the bonnie sparklin' glasses, as it is wi' poor Billy, it's then ye aye need a man wi' a good grip beside ye."

"What do you do then, Geordie?" I asked.

"Ow ay, I jist go for a wee walk wi' the lad, and then puts the kettle on and makes a cup o' tea or coffee, an' off he goes to sleep like a bairn."

"Poor Billy," I said. "Is there hope for him?"

"Hoot awa, man," said Geordie quickly. "Ye wouldna keep oot a poor creature frae creepin' in that's doin' his best?"

"But, Geordie," I replied, "he doesn't know anything about the doctrines. I don't think he could give you 'The Chief End of Man' from the first page of the Catechism."

"Ay," said Geordie sadly. "Tis weel enough for you and me who learned o' oor Scottish traditions when we was bairns. But poor Billy's had nae such a fine education. And surely ye canna hae forgotten the prood Pharisee and the poor wuman that came creepin' in behind the Maister."

The mingled tenderness and sternness in Geordie's face were beautiful to see. So I meekly answered, "Well, I hope Mr. Craig will be equally lenient with the boys."

Geordie shot a suspicious glance at me, but I kept my face. Then he replied cautiously—

"Ay, he's no that strict. But he must exercise discrimination."

Geordie was none the less determined, however, that Billy should eventually come all the way—which to him meant lining up with all the doctrines of the Scottish Shorter Catechism and the Established Kirk. But as to the manager, who was a member of the Church of England, and some others who had been confirmed years ago, and had forgotten much and denied more, he was extremely doubtful and expressed himself in very decided words to the minister—

"Ye'll be gettin' no support frae them Epeescopawlyuns. They ken naethin' aboot the true path."

But Mr. Craig looked at him for a moment, then said, " 'Him that cometh unto Me I will in no wise cast out,' " and Geordie was silent. Though he continued doubtful.

Even with all these divisive factions, however, there was no mistaking the earnest spirit of the men. The meetings grew larger every night, and the interest in spiritual things became more intense. The singing became different. The men no longer simply shouted, but as Mr. Craig would call attention to the meaning of the words of the hymn, the voices would attune themselves to the words. Instead of encouraging emotional excitement, Mr. Craig seemed to fear it.

"These chaps are easily stirred up," he would say, "and I am anxious that they should know exactly what they are doing. It is far too serious a business to trifle with. If they're going to give their hearts and lives to the service of the Lord, they can't walk far on emotions. It must go deeper."

Although Graeme, still recovering, did not go downstairs to the meetings, he could not but feel the throb of the new spiritual pulse beating in the heart of the community. I would tell him the incidents of each night, for his benefit and sometimes for his amusement. But I never felt quite easy in dwelling upon the humorous features of various conversations in Mrs. Mavor's presence, although Craig did not appear to mind. His manner with Graeme was perfect. Openly anxious to win him to his side, he did not try to improve his position with exhortation. He would not take him at a disadvantage, though, as I afterward found out, this was not the sole reason for his soft-spoken method. Mrs. Mavor, too, showed herself in a wise and tender light. She might easily have been his sister. She was so frank and openly affectionate, laughing at his anxieties and soothing his weariness.

There were never better comrades than we four, and the bright days speeding so swiftly on drew us nearer to one another.

But the bright days came to an end, for once Graeme was able to get up and move about, he became anxious to get back to his camp. And so the last day came; a day I remember well. It was a clean, crisp, winter day.

The air was shimmering in the frosty light. The mountains, with their shining heads piercing through light clouds into that wonderful blue of the western sky, and their feet pushed into the pine masses, gazed down upon Black Rock with calm, kindly looks on their old grey faces. How one grows to love those mountains, steadfast old friends!

Far up among the pines we could see the smoke of the engine at the works, and so still and so clear was the mountain air that we could hear the puff of the steam, and from far down the river the murmur of the rapids. The majestic silence, the tender beauty, the peace, the loneliness too, came stealing in upon us as we three, leaving Mrs. Mavor behind us, marched arm in arm down the street. We had not gone far on our way when Graeme turned around, stood a moment looking back, then waved his hand in farewell.

Mrs. Mavor was at her window, and she smiled and waved in return. They had grown to be great friends in a short span of time, and seemed to have arrived at some understanding. Certainly Graeme's manner to her was not that which he bore toward other women. His half-quizzical, somewhat superior air of mocking devotion gave place to a simple, earnest, almost tender respect, very new to him, but very winning.

As he stood there waving his farewell, I glanced at his face and saw for a moment something I had not seen for years, a faint flush on his cheek and a light of simple, earnest faith in his eyes. It reminded me of my first look at Graeme when we met at the University. He stood there on the campus looking up at the noble old buildings, and there was the same bright, trustful, earnest look on his boyish face.

I don't know what spirit came over me, but suddenly without thinking I blurted out, "It's no use, Graeme, my boy. I would fall in love with her myself if I thought there was half a chance. But I fear there is none."

The flush on his face slowly darkened as he turned and said—

"It's not like you, Connor, to make such a remark. She won't fall in love unless—"

He stopped abruptly with his eyes upon Craig.

But Craig met him with unshrinking gaze, then quietly remarked, "Her heart is under the pines."

Then we moved on, each thinking his own thoughts, and guessing at the thoughts of the others.

We were on our way to Craig's cabin, and as we passed the saloon Slavin stepped out of the door with a wave. Graeme paused. "Hello, Slavin," he said. "It looks like I got rather the worst of it, didn't I?"

Slavin approached us and said earnestly, "It was a dirty trick altogether what they done to you. You'll not think I put them up to it?"

"No, no, Slavin," replied Graeme cheerfully. "You stood up like a man."

"And you beat me fair. It was a mean one that laid me out, and there's no grudge that I gots toward you."

"Well, perhaps we'll understand each other better after this, Slavin."

"I'll see that yer boys don't get no more than they ask for," said Slavin, backing away.

"And I hope that won't be much," put in Craig, but Slavin only grinned.

By the time we reached Craig's cabin Graeme was glad to rest in a comfortable chair. Craig made him a cup of tea, while I walked about, admiring the deft neatness of the minister's housekeeping, and the gentle, almost motherly way he had with Graeme.

In the talk that followed our conversation drifted toward the future, and Craig was soon sharing his ambitions with us. The railway was soon to come. The resources of the west of Canada were as yet mostly unexplored, but enough was known to assure a great future for British Columbia. As he talked his enthusiasm grew and carried us away. With the eye of a general he surveyed the country, fixed the strategic points which the Church must seize upon. Eight good men would hold the country from Fort Steele to the coast, and from Kootenay to Cariboo.

"The Church must be in with the railway," he said. "She must have a hand in the shaping of the country. We need more brave young men, missionary pioneers to this rugged land! If society crystalizes without the influence of Christianity, the country is lost, and British Columbia will be another trapdoor to the bottomless pit."

"What are you proposing?" I asked.

"Well, it has to start someplace. So why not organize a congregation here in Black Rock?"

"How many would you be able to get to join?"

"Don't know. Numbers aren't important."

"Seems pretty hopeless among these miners."

"Hopeless!" he cried. "There were only twelve of us at first to follow Him, and rather a poor lot they were. But He braced them up, and they conquered the world."

"But surely things are different now," said Graeme.

"Yes, of course. Things are different. But *He* is the

same!" His face had taken on an exalted look, and his eyes were gazing into faraway places.

"A dozen men in Black Rock with some real grip of Him would make things go. We'll get them too," he went on in growing excitement. "I believe that we'll get them. And you get a handful of committed men, dead set to follow Him wherever He leads and whatever He says to do, and the world can be turned upside-down again!"

"Look here, Craig," said Graeme impulsively, "if you organize a church, I'd like to join. I don't particularly believe in all your doctrines, but I'll be blowed if I don't believe in you."

Craig looked at him with wistful eyes and shook his head.

"It won't do, old chap," he said. "I could never hold you. Don't you see—*I'm* nothing! *I'm* not the Church! It'll do nobody any good for you to believe in *me*! You've got to have a grip of some One better than I am. Such a step can't be taken for my sake, not for any man's sake. And as much as I appreciate your support, I fancy you feel right now like you want to please me and do it for me."

"That I do, old fellow," said Graeme. "I'll do anything you say."

"That's kind of you, Graeme," replied Craig. "But that's why I won't say. The organization is not mine...it is my Master's."

"When are you going to begin?"

"We shall have a communion service in two weeks, and that will be the first roll call."

"How many do you think will answer your call?" I asked doubtfully.

"I know of three," he said quietly.

"Three!" replied Graeme in amazement. "There are two hundred miners and one hundred and fifty lumbermen. "You think it worthwhile to organize a congregation for only three out of all those!"

96

"It won't be elaborate," said Craig, smiling for the first time, "but it will be effective. Loyalty demands obedience, and like I said, the numbers aren't so important alongside that. Give me six loyal men, committed to the cause of Christ without reservation, and this country will be changed for two hundred miles in every direction."

Graeme and I looked at each other. We both could hear what Jim Craig was saying, but it was not until years later that we really came to grasp the deeper meaning of his words. I myself—and I suppose I speak for my friend as well —were too conscious of surface appearances to truly understand him. Yet Craig was undaunted, and seemed to derive great support from our interest, as shallow as I now see it was.

We sat long that afternoon talking, shrinking from the breaking up of the fellowship. We knew that we were about to conclude a chapter in our lives which we should delight to think about and linger over in after days. And in my own life there is but one time brighter than that one.

At last we said good-bye. And though many farewells have come in between that day and this, none is so vividly present to me as that between us three men. Graeme would go back to his lumber camp, and things would revert to their old ways. I supposed I would have to be on my way before long as well, yet something still drew me to this place. The air seemed full of something about to happen.

Craig's manner with me when we parted was solemn enough. "Don't trifle with this," was what he said to me. But when he turned to Graeme his whole face lit up. He took him by the shoulders and gave him a little shake, looking into his eyes and saying over and over—

"You'll come, old chap, you'll come!"

Graeme could say nothing in reply, but only looked at the minister. Then they silently shook hands and the two of us drove off in the wagon.

But after we had got over the mountain and into the

winding forest road on the way back to Graeme's lumber camp, the voice kept vibrating in my heart: "You'll come... you'll come," and there was a hot pain in my throat.

We said little during that drive to the camp. Graeme was thinking hard, and made no answer when I spoke to him two or three times. Finally, when we came to the deep shadows of the pine forest, with a little shiver he said—

"It's all a tangle—a hopeless tangle."

"Meaning what?" I asked.

"This business of religion. There's so many varieties—Nelson's, Geordie's, Billy Breen's—if he has any—then Mrs. Mavor—she is a saint, of course—and that fellow Craig's. What a trump he is!—and without his religion he'd be pretty much like the rest of us. It is too much for me!"

9.
AN OLD STORY IN A STABLE

The gleam of the grand fire through the windows of the great camp hall gave a kindly welcome as we drove into the clearing in which the shanties stood.

Graeme was greatly touched at his enthusiastic welcome by the men. At the supper table he made a little speech of thanks for their faithfulness during his absence, especially commending the care and efficiency of Mr. Nelson, who had had charge of the camp.

The men cheered wildly, Baptiste's shrill voice leading them all. Nelson being called upon, he expressed a few words of pleasure in seeing the Boss back, and thanked the men for their support while he had been in charge.

The men were in a celebrating mood and proceeding to make a night of it. I feared the effect upon Graeme, for his thoughtful mood had continued. I spoke to Nelson, who passed the word, and in a short time the camp was quiet. As we sauntered from the grub-camp to the office, where Graeme slept and where I had made my bed during my stay with him, we paused to take in the beauty of the night. The moon rode high over the peaks of the mountains, flooding the narrow valley with mellow light. Under its magic the rugged peaks softened their harsh lines and seemed to lean lovingly toward us. The dark pine masses stood silent as in breathless adoration. The dazzling snow lay like a garment over all the open spaces in soft waving folds, crowning every stump with a quaintly shaped nightcap. The smoke curled up from the camp fires, standing like pillars of cloud that kept watch while men slept. And high over all the deep blue night sky, with its star jewels, sprang like the roof of a great cathedral from range to range, covering us in its kindly shelter.

How homelike and safe seemed the valley with its mountain sides, its sentinel trees and arching roof of jeweled sky! Even the night seemed kindly, and friendly the stars. And the lone cry of the wolf from the deep forest seemed like the voice of a comrade.

"How beautiful it all is!" said Graeme. "A night like this takes the heart right out of me."

I stood silent, drinking in the pleasures of the night with every one of my senses.

"What is it I want?" he went on. "Why does the night seem to make my heart ache? There are things to see and things to hear out there just beyond me. I cannot seem to get to them."

The gay, careless look was gone from his face, his dark eyes were wistful with yearning.

"Life must have something better for me," he continued, with the heartache still in his voice. "I have never been dissatisfied before. I love my life here in the mountains. Yet now, all of a sudden..."

His voice trailed off. I knew he had no more words. He did not even know himself what he was thinking and feeling.

I said nothing, but put my arm within his. In the quiet beauty of that night, something bound us together, and there was no embarrassment in such a show of manly affection.

A light appeared in the stable. "What's that?" I said,

glad for a diversion, for I did not know what to say to my friend in his present mood. "Let's go see."

"Sandy taking a last look at his team, likely enough," replied Graeme.

We walked slowly toward the stable, neither of us speaking again. As we neared the door we heard the sound of a voice in the monotone of one reading.

I stepped forward and looked through a chink between the logs of the building. Graeme was about to open the door, but I held up my hand and beckoned him to me.

In a vacant stall of the stable, there was a pile of clean straw upon which a number of men were grouped on the floor. Sandy, leaning against the tying-post upon which the stable lantern hung, was reading. Nelson was kneeling in front of him and gazing into the gloom beyond. Baptiste lay on his stomach, his chin in his hands and his upturned eyes fastened upon Sandy's face. Lachlan Campbell sat with his hands clasped about his knees, and two other men sat near him.

Sandy was reading from a Bible the story of the Prodigal, Nelson now and then stopping him to make a remark.

It was a scene I have never been able to forget. Today as I pause in my tale, I can still see that sight as clearly as when I looked through the chink in the logs upon it so many years ago. The long, low stable, with log walls and upright hitching posts. The dim outlines of the horses in the gloom of the background, and the little group of rough, almost savage-looking men, with faces wondering and reverent, lit by the misty light of the stable lantern.

After the reading, Sandy handed the book to Nelson, who put it in his pocket saying, "That's for us, ain't it, boys?"

"Ay," said Lachlan. "I hae heard it often, but I am afraid the ending o' the story winna be for me." He swayed himself slightly as he spoke, and his voice was full of pain.

101

"The minister said *I* might come," said old Nelson, earnestly and hopefully. "You can't be a worse prodigal than me."

"Ay, but you are not Lachlan Campbell, and ye've nae had his privileges. My ain father was an elder in the Free Kirk o' Scotland, and there was ne'er a night or morning but we took oor readings frae the Book."

"Yes," persisted Nelson, putting his hand on Lachlan's knee, "but he said *any man.*"

Still Lachlan shook his head.

"Dat young feller," said Baptiste. "What's his name?"

"He has no name. It's just a parable," explained Sandy.

"He's got no name?" asked Baptiste anxiously. "What can it mean den?"

Nelson took him in hand and explained to him the meaning of the parable insofar as he had applied it to God's acceptance of himself after so many years, telling him what had happened to him on Christmas eve. All the while Baptiste listened even more eagerly.

When Nelson had finished he broke out, "Ah, bon! Dat young feller, his name Baptiste, eh! And de old Father, he's le bon Dieu? Bon! Dat good story for me! But how you go back? How you go back to de Father? You go to priest?"

"The book says nothing about a priest or anyone else," said Nelson. "You go back in yourself, you see?"

"Non..." said Baptiste, clearly thinking over Nelson's words, trying to make sense out of them. The reality of the old story was entirely new to him. "Ah," he began to say as Nelson explained further—as if a light was beginning to break in upon him—"you go back *in your own self*. You make one leetle prayer. You say, 'Le bon Dieu, my Father, oh! I want come back to you. I so tire, so hongree, so sorree that I wander without you all these years."

"That's right," encouraged Nelson. "That's what I did."

"And He say, 'Come right along!' Dat what He say?"

"Yes, just like the father in the story. He's there all along with open arms, just waiting for us."

"Ah, bon! Dat first rate! Nelson, you make one leetle prayer for Sandy and me, right now?"

With neither hesitation nor embarrassment, Nelson lifted up his face and said, "Father, we're all gone far away. We have spent everything. We are poor, we are tired of it all. We want to feel different, to *be* different. We want to come back. Jesus came to save us from our sins, and He said if we came back He wouldn't cast us out, no matter how bad we were, if only we came to Him. Oh, Jesus Christ"—

His old, hard, iron-like face began to work, and two big tears slowly came from under his eyelids. He was clearly recalling his own experience in the snow from weeks earlier. "—We are a poor lot," he went on, "and I'm the worst of the outfit, and we are trying to find our way back. Show us how to get back to you. Amen."

"Bon!" said Baptiste. "Dat fetch Him sure!"

Graeme pulled me away, and without a word we went into the office and drew up to the little stove. Graeme was greatly moved.

"Did you ever see anything like that?" he asked. "Old Nelson! The hardest, most savage, toughest old sinner in the camp, on his knees praying in front of a bunch of men!"

"And in front of God," I could not help saying, for the old man evidently felt himself talking to someone. The scene had moved me, too.

"Yes, I suppose you're right," said Graeme doubtfully. "But there's so much about the whole thing I can't swallow."

He seemed to be thinking, then after a few moments went on.

"It seems the right sort of thing for some sorts. Take Lachlan. He's a Highland mystic. If he came out with visions, no one would think anything of it, least of all me. And Sandy's almost as bad. And Baptiste is an impulsive little chap. Those don't count much. But old man Nelson is a cool-blooded, levelheaded old fellow. And a mean cuss, too, in his day. He has seen a lot of life. And then there's Craig. He has a better head than I have, and is as hot-blooded. And yet he is living and slaving away in that hole Black Rock, and seems to really enjoy it. It all begins to look like there must be something in it."

"Of course there's something in it," I burst out, my own emotions over the events of the evening at last coming to the fore. "There's everything in it! If it's good enough for a trump like Craig, as you call him, and for a sweet lady like Mrs. Mavor, and for an old sinner like Nelson, and all the rest of them, how can it not be good enough for the likes of you and me? The trouble with me is, I can't face the music. It calls for a life where a fellow must go in for straight, steady work, self-denial, and that sort of thing. I'm too lazy for that. I don't know if I'm cut out for that kind of life. But that fellow Craig, as much as I like him, makes one feel horribly uncomfortable with his own drive and vision."

Graeme put his head to one side and looked at me curiously, as if examining me.

"I believe you're right about yourself," he said with a wry grin. "You always were a bit of a lazy beggar. But that's not where it catches me."

"Where then?" I asked.

But my friend did not answer. I knew it was a struggle he had to bear alone.

We sat and talked of other things for perhaps an hour and then turned in. Just as I was dropping off to sleep, I was roused by Graeme's voice—

"Are you going to Craig's preparatory service on Friday night?"

"Don't know," I replied rather sleepily.

"I say, do you remember the preparatory service at home, at the beginning of every school year?" There was something in his voice that set me wide awake.

"Yes. Rather a high spot, wasn't it?"

"He always mixed some religion in with it then, too. A little like Craig."

"I always felt better after it," I replied. "Ready to spring into action."

"To me"—he was sitting up in bed now—"to me it was like a call to arms, or rather like a call for a forlorn hope. None but volunteers wanted. No guarantees for an easy time of it. Hard work! Do you remember the thrill in the old governor's voice as he dared any but those with the right stuff to come along?"

"We'll go into town on Friday night," I said.

And so we did.

10.
FIRST ROLL-CALL OF THE
BLACK ROCK CHURCH

That Friday found many of us from Graeme's Lumber Camp Number 2 heading back down the mountain into Black Rock. Sandy took a load of men with his team, and Graeme and I drove in the light sleigh. By this time my plans to leave Black Rock were all but a memory. I had become a part of this place, and it had become a part of me.

The meeting was held in the church, and over a hundred men were present. There was some singing of familiar hymns at first, and then Mr. Craig read the same story as we had heard in the stable, that most perfect of all parables, the Prodigal Son. Baptiste nudged Sandy in delight, and whispered something, but Sandy held his face so absolutely expressionless that Graeme said—

"Look at Sandy. Something must have hit him hard."

The men were held fast by the story. The voice of the reader—low, earnest, and thrilling with the tender pathos of the tale—carried the words to our hearts, while a glance, a gesture, a movement of the body gave us the vision of it all as he was seeing it.

Then in the simplest of words he went on to tell us what the story meant, holding us all the while with his eyes and voice and gestures. Besides being a man anyone could be proud to call a friend, Jim Craig was one of the most compelling speakers I have ever heard, and his voice kept us spellbound.

He urged us to scorn the frivolous, heartless selfishness of the young fool setting forth so recklessly from the broken home. He moved our pity and our sympathy for the young prodigal, who, broken and deserted, still had pluck enough to determine to work his way back, and who, in utter desperation, at last gave up his fight. And then he showed us the homecoming—the ragged, heart-sick tramp, with hesitating steps, stumbling along the dusty road, and then the rush of the old father, his garments fluttering, and his voice heard in broken cries. It was no mere story. Craig made us *see* every detail! I can see and hear it all now, whenever the words are read.

Then he announced a hymn. It was called *Just As I Am*. He read the first verse: *Just as I am without one plea, but that thy blood was shed for me. and that thou bid'st me come to Thee, O Lamb of God, I come, I come.*

Then he went on to say, "There you are, men, every man of you, somewhere on the road. Some of you are too lazy"—here Graeme nudged me—"and some of you haven't got enough yet of the far country in you to come back. May there be a chance for you when you want to come! Men, you all want to go back home, and when you go you'll want to put on your soft clothes. And you won't till you can go in good style. But where did the prodigal get his good clothes? Surely not from the swine pit."

Quick came the answer in Baptiste's shrill voice—
"From de old fadder!"

No one was surprised to hear him, and the minister went on—

"Yes! and that's where *we* must get the good, clean

107

heart, the good, clean, brave heart—from our Father. Don't wait, but, just as you are, come. Now let's sing the hymn."

He led off, and they sang. Not loud and boisterous, but in voices subdued, holding down the emotions rising within them.

After the singing, Craig stood a moment gazing out at the men, and then said quietly—

"Does any man want to come? You *all* might come. We all *must* come!"

Then, sweeping his arm over the audience, and turning half round as if to move off, he cried, in a voice that thrilled to the heart's core—

"Oh! Come on, men! Let's go back home!"

The effect was overpowering. It seemed to me that the whole company half rose to their feet. Of the prayer that immediately followed, I only caught the opening sentence, "Father, we are coming back," Craig prayed in a loud voice, but my attention was suddenly absorbed by Abe, the stage-driver, who was sitting next to me. I could hear him saying to himself—

"Ain't he a clinker! I'll be gee-whizzly-goldusted if he ain't a malleable-iron-double-back-action self-adjusting corn-cracker!"

And as Craig went on, the prayer continued to be punctuated with similar admiring and even more sulphurous expletives.

It was such an incongruous medley. Nothing the like of it would ever be heard in any Eastern church! But this was the West, and a rough, frontier West at that. These were men with no eye nor ear for convention or regulation or appearances. These were men who were what they were, and tried to be nothing else—honest, hard-working, hard-drinking, hard-swearing but *real* men who now found their emotions and their hearts and their spiritual beings moved in ways they never dreamed possible. And they made no effort to

108

subdue the rising tide of responses coming forth from within them.

As a result, Craig's earnest, reverent prayer was mingled with sounds of many kinds—here and there a groan, an occasional "Amen," and even the earnest, admiring profanity, rendering chaotic all one's former ideas of so-called religious propriety. Yet I could not help but think that the feelings of both Craig as he prayed, and the men as their heart-feelings erupted out of their mouths, were somehow both akin. Though the method of expression was certainly widely diverse.

After the prayer, Craig's tone changed completely. In a quiet, matter-of-fact way he stated his plan to organize a church. Not just a building—they already had that. But a real church, a congregation, a company of believers committed together to a cause. Then he called for all who wished to join to remain after the benediction. Some fifty men were left, among them Nelson, Sandy, Lachlan Campbell, Baptiste, Shaw, Nixon, Geordie, and Billy Breen, who had tried to get out but was held fast by Geordie.

Graeme was on his way out, but I signaled him to remain, saying that I wished to "see the thing out." Abe sat still behind me, swearing disgustedly at the fellows leaving "who were going back on the preacher." Craig himself appeared amazed at the number of men remaining.

But as he began to address the new, smaller crowd, he did nothing to try to entice them by easy words. He put before them the terms of discipleship, as the Master did to the eager scribe, and he did not make them easy. He pictured the kind of work to be done, and the kind of men needed for the doing of it. Abe grew uneasy as the minister went on to describe the completeness of the surrender, the intensity of the loyalty demanded.

"That knocks me out of it, I reckon," he muttered in a disappointed tone. "I ain't up to that grade."

Craig went on to describe the heroism called for, the

magnificence of the fight, the worth of it all in the end, and the outcome of it if we could succeed—both the blessings to be had by giving one's heart to the Lord, and the good to the community and the whole area, of a thriving church where truth was taught. And at his words of enthusiasm, Abe finally blurted out' "I'll be blanked if I wouldn't like to take a hand in it, but I don't see how I can get in the game."

Craig finished his appeal by saying—

"I want to put this quite fairly. It is not any league of mine. You're not joining my company. It is no easy business, and it is for your whole life. What do you say? Do I put it fairly? What do you say, Nelson?"

Nelson rose slowly, and with some difficulty began—

"I may be all wrong. But all I can say is you made it easier for me, Mr. Craig. You said He would see me through, or I should never have risked it. You never said all this about complete surrender to me that night. You said Jesus would save me from my sins, and that He would see me through, even if I was weak myself. Perhaps I am wrong..." The old man looked troubled as he struggled for words.

Craig sprang up. "No! No!" he said. "Thank God, He will see every man through who will trust his life to Him. All I've been trying to do tonight is to keep the men from coming, thinking this was going to be like joining a club. But you are right! He *will* give you strength. He will do that for every man, no matter how tough he is, no matter how broken, no matter what he has done, no matter how far from home he has strayed."

Then Nelson straightened himself up and said—

"Well, sir! I can vouch for it then. I can tell you men that what the preacher says is true. It worked for me. He helped me through." Then, turning halfway round toward Craig, he added, "I believe a lot of the men would go in for this if they were dead sure they would get through."

"Get through!" said Craig. "Never a fear of it! It is a hard fight, a long fight, a glorious fight. But the fight is not ours. The battle over Black Rock is not Craig's or Nelson's or anyone else's. It is the Lord's! And every man who squarely trusts Him, and takes Him as Lord and Master, comes out the victor!"

"Bon!" cried Baptiste. "You tink He's take me in dat fight, M'sieu Craig?" His eyes were blazing.

"You mean it?" asked Craig almost sternly.

"Yes!" said the little Frenchman eagerly. "For sure!" and Craig wrote his name down.

Poor Abe looked amazed and distressed. He rose slowly, and saying, "That jars my whisky jug," walked out of the church. There was a slight movement near the organ, and glancing up I saw Mrs. Mavor put her face hastily in her hands. The men's faces were anxious and troubled, and Nelson said in a voice that broke—

"Tell them what you told me, sir."

But Craig replied, "You tell them, Nelson."

Nelson then began, with no hesitation now, and told the story of how he had begun just five weeks ago, about how he had really "heard" Craig's words on the night of Christmas Eve about the baby Jesus, and about what had passed between the two men later outside in the snow. The old man's voice steadied as he went on, and he grew eager as he told how he had been helped, and how the world was all different, and his heart seemed new. He spoke of Jesus as a new Friend as if He were someone that could be seen out at camp, that he knew well, and met everyday.

But as he tried to say how deeply he regretted that he had not known all this years before, the old, hard face began to quiver, and the steady voice wavered. Then he pulled himself together, and said—

"I feel sure He'll pull me through. Do you hear me, boys? *Me*! The hardest old man in these mountains! So don't you fear, boys! When the preacher talks about Jesus Christ helping you out and giving you a hand in all this, you can depend on it. He's all right!"

He resumed his seat and the gate was suddenly opened. The men began to come forward and give Craig their names. When it came to Geordie's turn, he gave his name—

"George Crawford, frae the parish o' Kilsyth, Scotland. And ye must jist put doon the lad's name wi' mine, Maister Craig. He's a wee bit troubled wi' the discourse, but he had the root o' the matter in him, I dinna doobt." And so Billy Breen's name went down as well.

When the meeting was over, thirty-eight names stood upon the roll of the Black Rock Presbyterian Church. And it will ever be one of the regrets of my life that neither Graeme's name nor my own appeared on that roll. And three days later, when the cup went around on that first Communion Sunday, from Nelson to Sandy, and from Sandy to Baptiste, and so on down the line to Billy Breen and Mrs. Mavor, and then to Abe the driver, whom she had, in those three days by her own mystic power, lifted into hope and faith, I felt all the shame and pain of a traitor, without courage enough to take the stand that these men had taken. And I believe in my heart that the fire of that pain and shame burned something of the selfish cowardice out of me, and that it is burning still.

The last words of the minister, in the short sermon following the communion service, were low and sweet and tender. But they were words of high courage. And before he had spoken them all, the men were listening with shining eyes. And when they rose to sing the closing hymn, they stood straight like soldiers on parade.

And I wished more than ever that I was one of them.

11.
THE SPRING OF 1883

There is no doubt in my mind that nature designed me to be a great painter. With apologies to my ego, perhaps I should only say greater than I became.

Whatever the design of nature and the God who made it, a railway director interfered with that plan. By the transmission of an order for mountain pieces by the dozen, together with a check so large I feared there was some mistake, he determined to make me an illustrator and designer for railway and like publications.

I do not take pleasure in these people ordering "by the dozen." Why can they not consider an artist's finer feelings? Perhaps they cannot understand them. But they understood my pictures, and I understood their checks, and there we were at a stand-off.

So it came that I remained in Black Rock throughout the Spring of 1883, working on my "dozen" illustrations—I cannot in good conscience call them *paintings*—and thus witnessed continuing changes in the small mining and lumber community.

Because of the nature of the work, there were always

new men coming in and others leaving. The community was therefore always in something of a state of flux. And this could not help but place the League, as well as the newly formed congregation under Jim Craig's leadership, in a sometimes precarious position as regarded the resolve of the men. A great ball planned for the week of Easter in April proved to be a turning point of sorts, though not of the kind which Craig would have hoped for.

The promoters of the ball determined that it should be a ball rather than a dance, and this was taken by the League men as a concession to the new public opinion in favor of respectability created by the League. And when the manager's patronage had been secured (they failed to get Mrs. Mavor's), it was further announced that, though held in the Black Rock Hotel ballroom—indeed, there was no other place and the word calling to mind luxurious appointments was not used without a good deal of irony—refreshments suited to the peculiar tastes of League men would be provided. It was felt to be almost a necessity that the League should approve, should indeed welcome, this concession to the public opinion in favor of respectability created by the League.

There were men taking extreme positions on both sides, of course. One of the newcomers, "Idaho" Jack, professional gambler, for instance, frankly considered that the whole town was going to unmentionable depths of ridiculous propriety unbefitting men altogether. Craig's influence had done nothing to move him, and he regarded the organization of the League—and he was not alone in this view—as a sad retrograde toward the bondage of the ancient ways of the East. If he could not get drunk when and where he pleased, "Idaho," as he was called, would regard it as a personal grievance.

Idaho was of a rough breed and didn't particularly care for all the religious notions he found being talked about by some of the men. In fact, he was not enamored of the social

114

way of Black Rock at all. He was outright disgusted when he learned that guns were not allowed, and had been decreed by law to be an unnecessary adornment of a card table. The night on which he made this discovery must have been a memorable one in the saloon.

As the story went, Idaho was industriously pursuing his avocation in Slavin's with his gun lying next to him on the card table, convenient to his hand and acting as a visible deterrent against any thought of trying to cheat him. In walked policeman Jackson, her Majesty's sole representative in the Black Rock district, who looked around, and then focused his attention on the table in question. Stonewall Jackson, or "Stonewall" as he was called, watched the game for a few moments, then walked slowly forward, reached out, tapped the pistol lightly with the end of his stick, and asked what this was used for.

"I'll show you in two minutes if you don't light out," spat Idaho angrily, hardly glancing up. The luck had been running against him and he had just missed drawing to a straight and was holding nothing, with five of his own dollars sitting in the pile in the middle of the table.

Jackson tapped upon the table, then said in a sweet and kindly voice—

"You're a stranger here. You ought to watch what you say and who you say it to. Now, the boys here know I don't interfere with an innocent little game. But there is a regulation against playing it with guns. So," he went on, even more sweetly, but fastening Idaho with a look from his steel-grey eyes, "I'll just take charge of this."

He picked up the revolver, and added, "You never know when it might go off."

Idaho half jumped from his chair in rage. But his anger was quite swallowed up in his amazement, taken so off guard as he was, at the state of a society that would allow such an outrage upon personal liberty. He stammered, swore a little, but was quite unable to play anymore that evening.

It took several drinks all round to restore him to articulate speech. The rest of the night was spent in retaining for his instruction stories of the ways of Stonewall Jackson.

Idaho bought a new gun, but he wore it around his waist, never placed it on a card table, and used it chiefly in the pastime of shooting out the lights or in picking off the heels from the boys' boots while a stag dance was in progress in Slavin's. But in Stonewall's presence, Idaho remained a most respectable citizen.

Stonewall was a man Idaho could understand. He was six feet three, and had an eye of unpleasant penetration. But this new regard in the community for respectability he could *not* understand, nor endure. The League became the object of his indignant aversion, and the League men targets of his contempt. He had many sympathizers, for Slavin's regular customers outnumbered Craig's ranks by at least two to one. Frequent were Idaho's verbal assaults on the newly-born sobriety of Billy Breen and others of the League.

But Geordie's watchful care and Mrs. Mavor's steady influence, together with the loyal cooperation of the rest of the League men, kept Billy safe for a good while. Besides Billy, Nixon too was a marked man. Idaho determined within himself to "win him back." It may be that he carried himself with unnecessary jauntiness toward Slavin and Idaho, saluting the former with, "Awful dry weather! eh, Slavin?" and the latter with, "Hello, old sport! How's times?" causing them to swear deeply at him. And as it turned out, to do more than swear.

But on the whole the anti-League men were in favor of a respectable ball, and most of the League men determined to show their appreciation of the concession of the committee to the principles of the League in the important matter of refreshments by attending in force.

Nixon, however, said he would not go. However carefree may have been his appearance when walking down the street, he said he could not trust himself where whisky was flowing. For it got into his nose "like a fish-hook into a salmon." He was from Nova Scotia.

For similar reasons, Vernon Winton, the young Oxford fellow, determined not to go. When the men goaded him, his lips grew a little thinner, and the color deepened in his handsome face, but he went on his way.

Geordie despised the whole notion of the ball as a "daft ploy," and the spending of five dollars on a ticket he considered a "sinful waste o' guid siller." And he warned Billy against "coontenancing any sich rideeklus nonsense."

The last two months had done wonders for Billy's personal appearance, and for his position in the social scale as well. Everyone knew what a fight he was making, and esteemed him accordingly. Thus no one expected him to go.

How well I remember the pleased pride in his face when he told me about the ball committee's request that he should join the orchestra with his fiddle. It was not simply that his violin was his pride and joy, but he felt their request to be a recognition of his return to respectability.

I have often marveled at how little, seemingly accidental, details combine for great effect upon the ways of man.

Had Mr. Craig not been away at the Landing that week, had Geordie not been on the night-shift at the mine, and had Mrs. Mavor not been so preoccupied with the care of her sick child, it may be that Billy might have been saved his fall.

The anticipation of the ball stirred up the emotions in Black Rock all the week beforehand with a thrill of expectant delight. I must admit that I too, viewed the approaching evening with pleasurable anticipation. The eagerness of the men was scarcely to be wondered at, considering for how many weeks on end, seven days following upon seven days, they would swing their picks in the dark holes of the mines, or chop and saw among the solitary silences of the great forests. Any break in the long and weary monotony of their hard-working lives was welcome indeed. And who thought to consider the cost or consequence!

To even the simplest and least cultured of them, the dreary tedium of the life must have been hard to bear. But what this strenuous life, without break, without entertainment, without a wider ranger of persons to talk to, must have been to those few of the men who had seen life in its more cultured and attractive forms, I can hardly imagine. From the mine, black and foul, to the shacks where they lived, bare and cheerless and sometimes hideously repulsive and filthy, their lives swung back and forth in heart-grinding monotony. They were paid well enough for their exhausting labors, but not so well that they could hope to climb out of the social hole such work inevitably placed them in.

The work, the boredom, the exhaustion went on, day after day, week after week, until the longing for a "big drink" or some other big "event" became too great to bear.

And so approached the night of the ball.

12.
THE BREAKING OF THE LEAGUE

It was well on toward the evening of Good Friday when Sandy's four-horse team, with a load of men from the woods, came swinging round the curves of the mountain-road and down the street.

A gay crowd they were with their bright, brown faces and hearty voices. In ten minutes the whole street seemed alive with lumbermen—they had a knack of spreading themselves about and enlivening the town whenever they came down to Black Rock.

After night fell the miners came in "done up slick." This was a great occasion and their dress must be up to it. The manager appeared in evening dress, but most of the men voted this a mite "too giddy."

As Graeme and I walked up to the Black Rock Hotel, we met old man Nelson looking very grave.

"Going, aren't you, Nelson?" I said.

"Yes," he answered slowly. "I'll drop in, though I don't like the look of things much."

"What's the matter, Nelson?" asked Graeme cheerily. "There's no funeral on."

119

"Maybe not," replied Nelson, "but I can't help wishing Mr. Craig were home." Then he added, "When Idaho and Slaviñ get together, you can bet the devil isn't far off."

Graeme laughed, and we passed on. As we walked into the large storeroom—the so-called ballroom—where the ball was to be held, the orchestra was turning up. Billy Breen was lovingly fingering his instrument, now and then indulging himself in a little snatch of some tune that came to him out of his happier past. He looked perfectly delighted, and as I paused to listen he gave me a proud glance out of his deep, little blue eyes, and went on playing softly to himself.

Presently Shaw came along.

"That's good, Billy," he called out. "You've still got the touch, I see."

Billy only nodded and went on playing.

"Where's Nixon?" I asked.

"Gone to bed," said Shaw, "and I am glad of it. He finds that the safest place on the afternoon of a payday. The boys don't bother him there."

The dancing room was lined on two sides with beer barrels and whisky kegs. The orchestra was positioned at one end, and at the other sat a table adorned with refreshments, where the "soft-drinks" might be had. Those who wanted anything else might pass through a short passage into the bar just behind.

This was evidently a superior kind of ball, for the men kept on their coats and went through the various figures with faces of unnatural solemnity. But the strain upon their feelings was quite apparent, and it became a question of how long it could be maintained. As the trips through the passageway became more frequent the dancing grew in vigor and hilarity, until by the time supper was announced the stiffness had sufficiently vanished to give no further anxiety to the committee.

But there were other causes for concern. After supper certain of the miners appeared with their coats off, and proceeded to "knock the knots out of the floor" in breakdown dances of extraordinary energy. Afterward they were beguiled into the bar room and filled up for safety. The committee had been determined that the respectability of the ball should be preserved to the end. Their reputation was at stake, not in Black Rock only, but at the Landing as well, from which most of the ladies had come. And to be shamed in the presence of the Landing people could not be tolerated.

But gradually difficulties seemed to be increasing, for at this point something seemed to be wrong in the orchestra, in the violin section. One of the instruments appeared to be wandering aimlessly up and down the scale, occasionally picking up the tune with animation, and then losing it again. As Billy saw me approaching, he drew himself up with great seriousness, gravely winked at me, and said—

"Shlipped a cog, Misther Connor! Most unfortunate! Beautiful instrument too, but shlips a cog. Mosh unforchunate!"

He wagged his little head sagely, playing all the while for dear life, now second and now lead.

Poor Billy! I could not help thinking of the beautiful, eager face that leaned toward him the night the League was made, and of the bright voice that said, "You'll sign with me, Billy?" It seemed a cruel deed to make him lose his grip of life and hope on an evening such as this. For that was what the pledge meant to him.

I made an effort to get Billy out of the orchestra and away to some safe place, but just then I heard a great shouting in the direction of the bar, followed by a trampling and scuffling of feet in the passageway. Suddenly a man burst through, crying out—

"Let me go! Stand back! I know what I'm about!"

It was Nixon, dressed in his best—black suit, blue shirt, red tie, looking handsome enough, but half-drunk and wildly excited. The Highland Fling competition was on at that moment, and Angus Campbell, Lachlan's brother, was re-

121

presenting the lumber camps in the contest. Nixon looked on for a few moments, then with a quick movement he seized the little Highlander, swung him in his powerful arms clean off the floor, and deposited him gently upon a beer barrel. Then he stepped into the center of the room, bowed to the judges, and began a sailor's hornpipe.

The committee was perplexed, but after talking it over decided to humor the new competitor, especially as they all knew that with whisky in him Nixon was an unpleasant man to cross.

Lightly and gracefully he went through his steps, the men crowding in from the bar to admire him, for Nixon was famed for his hornpipe. But when, after the dance, he proceeded to execute a clog-dance, garnished with acrobatic feats, the men of the committee interfered. There were cries of "Put him out!" and "Let him alone...go on Nixon!" And Nixon hurled two of the committee men back into the crowd when they tried to lay restraining hands upon him. Standing in the open center of the room, he cried out scornfully—

"You want to put me out! Help yourselves! Don't mind me!"

Then he ground his teeth, and added with savage deliberation, "If any man lays a finger on me, I'll—I'll eat his liver cold."

He stood for a few moments glaring round upon the company, and then strode purposefully toward the bar, followed by the wildly yelling growl. Instantly the ball was broken up. I looked around for Billy, but he was nowhere to be seen. Graeme touched my arm—

"There's going to be something of a time, so just keep your eyes open."

"What are you going to do?" I asked.

"Do? Keep myself out of trouble," he replied.

In a few minutes the crowd came surging back, led by Nixon who was waving a whisky bottle over his head and yelling as one possessed.

"Ah!" exclaimed Graeme softly. "I begin to see what is happening. Look...over there."

"What's up?" I asked.

"There's Idaho and Slavin, and their lackeys," he replied. "They've got poor Nixon in tow. They probably gave him his first drink and are now delighting in this."

"I thought you were going to keep out of it," I said.

"I've seen some of Idaho's work before," he answered. "I think I may reconsider and take a hand in this game after all."

The scene was a strange one to me, and was wild beyond description. A hundred men filled the room. Bottles were passed from hand to hand, and men drank their fill. Behind the refreshment tables stood the hotelman and his barkeeper with their coats off and sleeves rolled up to the shoulder, passing out bottles, and drawing beer and whisky from two kepts hoisted up for that purpose. Nixon was in his glory. It was his night. Every man was to get drunk at his expense, he proclaimed, flinging down bills on the table. Near him were some League men he was treating liberally, and never far away were Idaho and Slavin passing bottles around, but evidently drinking little themselves.

I followed Graeme, not feeling too comfortable, for this sort of thing was new to me. Yet I could not but admire the cool assurance with which he made his way through the crowd that swayed and yelled and swore and laughed in a most disconcerting manner.

"Hello!" shouted Nixon as he caught sight of Graeme. "Here you are!" he called out, passing him a bottle.

Graeme proposed that he should give the hornpipe again, hoping to distract the crowd somewhat. The floor was cleared at once, for Nixon's hornpipe was very popular, and tonight, of course, was in high favor. In the midst of the dance, however, Nixon stopped short, his arms dropped to his side, and his face was overcome with a look of fear and horror.

There in front of him, still in his riding clothes and boots, with his whip in his hand as he had come directly from his ride, stood Jim Craig. His face was pale, but his dark eyes were blazing with fierce light. As Nixon stopped, Craig stepped forward to him, and sweeping his eyes around upon the circle, he said in a tone of intense scorn—

"You cowards! You get a man where he's weak! Cowards! You won't let the fight be a fair one for fear you'll lose. Cowards! You'd damn a man's soul for a few dollars out of his pocket!"

There was a dead silence. Then Craig lifted his hat and said solemnly—

"May God forgive you this night's work!"

Finally, turning to Nixon, and throwing his arm over the man's shoulder, he said in a voice broken and husky—

"Come on, Nixon, let's get out of here!"

Idaho made a motion as if to stop him, but Graeme stepped quickly forward and said sharply, "Make way there, let them through," and the crowd fell back. Graeme and I followed the other two, Nixon walking as if in a dream, with Craig's arm about him. Down the street we went in silence, to Craig's cabin, where we found old man Nelson with the fire blazing, and strong coffee steaming on the stove. He had been the one to tell Craig of Nixon's fall the moment he arrived home.

There was not a word of reproach from the minister, only gentlest pity in tone and tender touch as Craig placed the half-drunk dazed man in his easy-chair, took off his boots, brought him his own slippers, and gave him a cup of coffee. Then, as his stupor began to overcome him, Craig put him in his own bed, and came out with a face written all over with grief.

"Don't worry about it, old chap," said Graeme kindly. "It was bound to happen to some of them."

But Craig looked at him without a word, and, throwing himself into a chair, put his face in his hands. As we sat there in silence, the door was suddenly pushed open and in walked Abe Baker with the words, "Where is Nixon?"

We told him he was in the other room asleep. We were still talking when again a tap came to the door, and Shaw came in with a distressed look on his face.

"Did you hear about Nixon?" he asked. We told him what we knew.

"But did you hear how they got him?" he asked.

As he told us the tale, the men stood listening with faces growing harder the more he told.

It appeared that after the making of the League the owner of the Black Rock Hotel had bet Idaho one hundred dollars to fifty that Nixon could not be induced to drink before Easter.

Idaho had taken up the challenge but thus far all his schemes had failed, and now he had only three days in which to win his money. The ball was his last chance. But here again he was foiled, for Nixon had resisted all entreaties to go, locking his cabin door and going to bed before nightfall, his custom on paydays.

At midnight some of Idaho's men came battering at the door for admission, which Nixon reluctantly granted. For half an hour they used every art of persuasion they could think of to induce him to go down to the ball. But Nixon remained immovable, and they finally left, baffled and cursing. In two hours they returned drunk enough to be dangerous, kicked at the door in vain, finally gained entrance through the window, hauled Nixon out of bed, held a glass of whisky to his lips, and made him drink. But he knocked the glass away, spilling the liquor over himself and the bed.

By this time it was drink or fight, and Nixon was ready to fight. But after a little discussion they had a drink all round, and fell to trying to persuade him again. The night was cold, and poor Nixon sat shivering on the edge of his bed. If he would take one drink they would leave him alone.

He didn't need to be so stiff.

The whisky fumes filled his nostrils. If one drink would get them away, surely that was better than fighting and killing someone or getting killed himself. He hesitated a moment longer, at length yielded, and drank his glass.

They did not leave, but continued to sit about, drinking amiably, and lauding him as a fine fellow after all. One more glass before they left. Then Nixon rose, dressed himself, drank all that was left of the bottle, put his money in his pocket, and came down to the dance, wild with his old-time madness, reckless of faith and pledge, forgetful of home, wife, babies, his whole being absorbed in one great passion—to drink and drink and drink till he could drink no more.

Before Shaw finished his tale, Craig's eyes were streaming with tears, and groans of rage and pity broke alternately from him. Abe remained speechless for a time, not trusting himself, but as he heard Craig groan, "The beasts!" he seemed encouraged to let himself loose, and he began swearing with the coolest and most blood-curdling deliberation. Craig listened with evident approval for a few moments, when suddenly he seemed to wake up. He caught Abe by the arm, and said in a horrified voice—

"Stop! God forgive us! We mustn't talk like this."

Abe stopped at once, and in a surprised and slightly grieved voice said—

"What's the matter? Ain't that what you wanted?"

"Yes, God forgive me! I'm afraid it was," he answered hurriedly. "But hatred and rage is not the way to conquer evil."

"Oh, don't you worry," Abe went on, "I'll look after the part of conquering them blankest blankety blank"—going off again into a roll of curses against Slavin and his men, till Craig succeeded again in stopping the flow of profanity possible to no one but a mountain stage-driver. Abe paused, looked puzzled for a moment, and asked if they did not deserve everything he was calling down upon them.

"Yes, yes," replied Craig, "but that is not our business. We must leave all that to the Lord and take no hand in vengeance ourselves."

"Well, so I reckon," replied Abe, reluctantly enough, recognizing at last the limitations of the cloth. "You ain't used to it, I suppose. But it just makes me feel good—like bein' let out o' school—to properly do 'em up, the blank, blank," and off he went again. It was only under the pressure of Craig's prayers and commands that he finally agreed to hold it in, though it was not easy.

As we were discusssing what should be done, outside we heard the approach of someone else, striding up at a great pace. Craig opened the door to see Geordie Crawford.

"Hae ye seen the lad?" were his only words.

No one replied. I told Geordie of my last sight of Billy in the orchestra, appearing as though he had been drinking.

"An' did ye no go after him?" he asked in surprise. "Ow! he'll be tumbled weel over the bank by noo!"

"Billy gone too!" lamented Shaw. "The least they might have done was let Billy alone."

Poor Craig stood in silent agony. Billy's fall seemed more than he could bear. We left him there in his cabin, amid the ruins of his League.

13.
GRAEME'S DANGEROUS PLAN

As we stood outside Craig's cabin in the dim starlight, we could not hide from ourselves the fact that the League had been badly beaten. But what could be done? The yells of carousing miners down at Slavin's told us that nothing could be done with them that night.

"I'd like to get back at 'em," said Abe, carefully repressing his language.

There was silence again for a few moments.

"I've got it, men," said Graeme suddenly. "This town does not require all the whisky that is in it by a long shot! Why don't we clear some of it out?"

His plan was to take possession of Slavin's saloon and the bar of the Black Rock Hotel, and, while keeping the men out, to empty as many of the bottles and casks as possible.

"We'd never pull it off," I objected. "They'd kill us before letting us pour out their precious liquor."

"We'll have to trick them, and do the deed in private."

"And just how do you propose to accomplish that?"

"Well, I'm gaein' after the lad," said Geordie. "I'll hae

naethin' to do wi' it. It winna be that easy, an' it's a sinful waste."

But Abe was wild to try it, Shaw was quite willing, while old man Nelson sternly approved. I therefore found myself an unwitting accomplice as well.

"Nelson, you and Shaw get a couple of our men and attend to the saloon. Slavin and the whole gang are up at the Black Rock so you won't have much trouble. But come to us as soon as you can."

And so we went our ways. I still didn't like it, but followed nevertheless. When Graeme was enthusiastic, one hardly thought of not jumping in all the way with him.

We had little difficulty getting the men out of the Hotel. Abe took a position in the middle of the street and began to yell frantically. Some men rushed outside to see what was causing the uproar. He seized the first man to approach him, continuing to make hideous sounds, and in three minutes had every man out of the hotel and a lively fight in progress out in the street.

In two minutes more Graeme and I had the door to the ballroom locked and barricaded with empty casks. We then closed the door of the bar room leading to the outside. The bar room was a strongly built log shack, with a heavy door secured after the manner of early pioneering cabins, with two strong oak bars, so that we felt safe from attack from that quarter.

We could not hope to hold the ballroom for long, for the door was not a heavy one, and entrance was possible through the windows. But as only a few casks of liquor were left there, our main work would be in the bar, so that the fight would be to hold the passageway. This we barricaded with casks and tables.

By this time the crowd had begun to realize that something sinister was going on, had turned back from the street to the Hotel, and were now wildly yelling at door and windows. With an axe which Graeme had brought with him, the ballroom casks were soon mutilated sufficiently and left to empty their priceless, destructive liquid themselves.

As I was about to empty the last cask, Graeme stopped me. "Let that stand there," he said. "It will help us. Now skip for the barricade!" he yelled, as a man came crashing through a window. Before he could regain his feet, however, Graeme had seized him and flung him out upon the heads of the crowd outside.

But men were coming in through the other windows, and Graeme rushed for the barricade, followed by two of the enemy, the first of whom I received at the top and hurled back upon the others. Most of the men were too drunk to have much control of themselves, and too dulled of perception to think clearly, and both these factors aided us in holding them off.

"Now, be quick!" said Graeme once we were in the bar room, "I'll hold them off from here. Break in the casks! But don't throw any bottles on the floor—throw them out there," he said, pointing to a little window high up in the wall, "and let them break outside."

I made all haste. The casks did not take much time, and soon the whisky and beer were flowing all over the floor, It made me think of Geordie's regret over the "sinful waste."

The bottles took longer, and as I tossed them up for the window, only missing once or twice, I glanced over and saw that Graeme was being hard pressed. Men would leap toward him two and three at a time, and up on the barricade. Graeme's arms would shoot out, and over the men would topple, senseless, onto the heads of those nearest. It was a great sight to see him standing alone with a smile on his face and the light of battle in his eye, coolly meeting his assailants with those terrific, lightning-like blows. Inside I was sure Jim Craig would not approve of our tactics, but I could not help but feel a certain glorious exuberance in fighting such a holy war of sorts.

In ten minutes my work was done.

"How do we get out?" I called.

"How is the door?" he replied.

I looked through the port-hole and said, "A crowd of men is waiting."

"We'll have to make a dash for it, I imagine," he replied cheerfully, though his face was already splotched with blood and his breath was coming in short gasps.

"Get down the bars and be ready."

But even as he spoke a chair was hurled from below and caught him on the arm. Before he could recover, a man had cleared the barricade and was upon him like a tiger.

It was Idaho Jack.

"Hold the barricade!" Graeme called out to me, as they both went down in a heap on the floor.

I sprang to his place, but had not much hope of holding it long. I had the heavy oak bar from the door in my hands, and swinging it round my head I made the crowd stand back for a few moments.

In the meantime Graeme had shaken off his enemy, who was circling about him with an evil glare, a long knife in his hand, waiting for a chance to spring. I had no doubt that in his angered state of intoxication, Idaho would kill Leslie in an instant if given half the chance.

"I have been waiting for this for some time, Mr. Graeme," he said with a wicked smile.

"No doubt ever since I spoiled your cut-throat game down in Frisco," replied Graeme. "How is the little one?" he added sarcastically.

Idaho's face immediately lost its smile, if such it could be called, and became distorted with renewed fury.

"She is—is—where you will be before I am done with you!" he replied, spitting out the words venomously.

"So, you murdered her too!" said Graeme. "I never knew for certain. You'll hang someday, Idaho—"

But he scarcely had time to get the words out, for at that instant Idaho sprang toward him.

Graeme dodged his blow and caught his forearm with his left hand, holding the murderous knife high in the air. Back and forth they swayed over the floor, slippery with whisky, the knife held out of reach by Graeme's strong grasp —but Idaho was made equally strong by the madness of his wrath, crazed with the effect of alcohol.

I wondered why Leslie did not strike him, but then I saw his right hand hanging limp from the wrist where he had apparently been hurt. The men were crowding upon the barricade. Despairing, I hardly knew what to do. They would kill us if given time!

I could tell Graeme's strength was going fast. Suddenly, with a yell of fury, Idaho gathered himself and threw his body upon Leslie with all its weight. Graeme could only cling to him. Together they staggered toward me where I still stood on the barricade.

Round and round they swayed, and as they fell I brought down my bar upon the upraised hand, hitting the wrist squarely and sending the knife flying across the room.

Idaho's howl of rage and pain was mingled with a shout from below. There, knocking the crowd right and left and dashing through them, came old Nelson, followed by Abe, Sandy, Baptiste, Shaw, and others. As they reached the barricade it crashed down, and carried me to the floor under the tumbling casks and furniture.

When I came to myself and looked out I saw a new danger. In the fall Graeme had wound his arms about the enemy and held him in a grip so fast that he was powerless to strike. But Graeme's strength was failing, and Idaho was slowly dragging himself, carrying Graeme on his back with him, across the floor toward the knife. Nearer and nearer his outstretched fingers came to the weapon.

In vain I yelled and struggled to free myself. But my voice was lost in the awful din and I could hardly hope to work myself free from the barrels and benches and chairs in time.

Above me, standing on a barrelhead, was Baptiste, yelling like a demon.

Desperately I called to him, but he could not hear me. Slowly Idaho was dragging his almost unconscious victim toward the knife. His fingers were just about to touch the point of the blade, when at last I was able to reach out and grab Baptiste's foot and gain his attention.

"Look! Look!" I cried. "Stop him!"

The fingers had closed upon the knife and Idaho had squirmed free enough to raise the knife high over Graeme's back, when, with a shriek, Baptiste cleared the room at a bound, and before the knife could fall the little Frenchman's boot had caught the uplifted wrist, and sent the knife flying again, this time clear to the wall.

Then there was a great rushing sound as of wind through the forest, and the lights went out.

When I awoke, I found myself lying with my head on Graeme's knees, and Baptiste sprinkling snow on my face to bring me around.

As I looked up, Graeme said—

"Good boy! It was a great fight, and we put it up well." Then he added, "I owe you my life, old chap."

His words thrilled my heart through, for I loved him as only men can love men. But I could only answer—

"I'm afraid I couldn't keep them back."

"It was well done. The best two could do against a drunken army," he said, and I felt proud.

I was indeed lucky to have gotten out of it so well. In that wild region it was not uncommon for men to lose their lives attempting something so foolhardy as we had done. As it was, Graeme got off with a bone in his wrist broken, and I with a couple of cracked ribs.

But had it not been for the open barrel of whisky which kept them occupied for a time, offering too good a chance to be lost, and for the timely arrival of Nelson and Baptiste, neither of us would have ever seen the light of day again.

14.
WHAT HAPPENED TO BILLY BREEN

We found Craig asleep on his couch.

When he woke, seeing us torn, bruised, and bloody, his consternation was almost laughable. But he hastened out of bed to find us warm water and bandages, and soon we felt as comfortable as our pain would allow.

Baptiste was radiant with pride over the fight, hovering about Graeme and me, all the while giving vent to his feelings in French and English expletives. Abe, however, was disgusted with himself, thinking he had failed at Slavin's. For when he and Nelson had gone to the saloon they had found Slavin's French-Canadian wife in charge of the place, with her baby on her lap. "We can't touch this," they had agreed, and had left without lifting a finger against all the alcohol remaining in the place. A baby held the fort.

As Craig listened to the account of the fight, he tried hard not to approve, but he could not keep the gleam out of his eyes. And as I pictured Graeme dashing back the crowd thronging the barricade till he was brought down by the chair, Craig laughed gently and put his hand on Graeme's knee. And as I went on to describe my agony while scream-

134

ing out the danger as Idaho's fingers were gradually nearing the knife, his face grew pale and his eyes wide.

"Baptiste here did the business," I said, and the little Frenchman nodded complacently and said—

"Dat's me for sure."

"Craig only smiled. "It was awfully risky," he said to Graeme, "and it seems hardly worth it. They'll get more whisky, and anyway, the League is as good as gone now."

"Well," said Graeme with a sigh of satisfaction, "at least it is not now quite such a one-sided affair as it was."

Nixon was snoring in the next room, and no one had heard of Billy, and there were others of the League that we knew were even at that moment down at Slavin's. It appeared that Craig's statement might not be so far from the truth. It was thought best that all should remain in Craig's cabin, not knowing what might happen if we went out again. So we lay where we could, and we needed no one to sing us to sleep.

When I awoke, stiff and sore, it was to find breakfast ready and old man Nelson in charge. When we were seated at the table, Craig came in, and I saw that he was not the disheartened man of the night before. His courage had come back, his face was quiet, and his eyes were clear. He was his own man again.

"Geordie has been out all night," he announced quietly, "but he has not been able to find Billy."

We did not talk much. Graeme and I were in bad enough shape with our broken bones, and the others suffered from a general morning depression. But when breakfast was over, as the men were beginning to move, Craig took down his Bible, and said—

"Wait a few moments, men!"

Then he began to read slowly, in his beautiful, clear voice, that psalm for fighters—

"God is our refuge and strength," and so on to "The Lord of Hosts is with us; the God of Jacob is our refuge."

135

The mighty words seemed to pull us together, lifting us till we grew ashamed of our rage.

Then Craig prayed in simple, straightforward words. He acknowledged, first of all, the failure, but I knew he was thinking chiefly of himself and not of anything the rest of us had done. Then he expressed gratitude for the men about him, and I felt my face growing hot with shame. And there followed a petition to the Lord for help, and we all thought of Nixon, and Billy, and all the other League men now walking from their debauch at Slavin's on this pure, bright morning. Finally he asked that we might be made faithful and worthy of God, whose battle it was.

When it was over we all stood up and shook hands with him in silence. Every one of us knew a covenant was being made then and there. But none saw his meeting with Nixon which followed. He sent us all away before he walked into the room where Nixon lay.

Nothing was heard of the destruction of the hotel's stock of liquor. Unpleasant questions would certainly be asked, and the proprietor decided to let it all go. On the point of respectability, the success of the ball was not conspicuous. But the anti-League men were content, if not jubilant.

Geordie found Billy Breen late in the afternoon in his old and deserted shack, breathing heavily, covered up in his filthy, molding blankets, with a half-empty bottle of whisky at his side. Geordie's combined grief and rage were beyond even his Scotch control. He spoke only a few words, but those were of such concentrated vehemence that no one felt the need of Abe's assistance in vocabulary.

Poor Billy! He was in desperate shape.

We carried him to Mrs. Mavor's, put him in a warm bath, then rolled him in blankets and proceeded to give him little sips of hot water, then progressing to hot milk and coffee. I had seen a clever doctor in the hospital treat a similar case of nerve and heart depression.

But it was seriously doubtful whether his already weakened system could recover from the shock of the exposure following his drunken binge. Finally on Sunday afternoon, Easter Day, we could tell that his heart was failing fast. All day the miners had been dropping in to ask about him, for Billy had been a great favorite in former days, and his recent fight against alcohol had captured the attention and admiration of the town. News of his condition was received with more than ordinary sorrow. As Mrs. Mavor sang to him, his large coarse hands moved in time to the music, but he did not open his eyes till he heard Craig's voice in the next room. Then he spoke his name, and in less than a moment Craig was kneeling beside him. The words came slowly—

"I tried to fight it out—but—I got beaten. It hurts to think—that *He's* ashamed o' me. Id like to a' done better—I would."

"Ashamed of you, Billy?" said Craig in a voice that was near breaking. "Not me."

"An'—ye all helped me so!" the poor lad went on. "I wish I'd done better!" and his eyes sought Geordie, and then rested on Mrs. Mavor, who smiled back at him with a world of love in her eyes.

"You ain't ashamed o' me—I can tell that from your eyes, ma'am," he said, gazing up at her.

"No, Billy," she said, and I wondered how she could keep her voice so steady, "not a bit. Why, Billy, I am proud of you."

He gazed up at her with wonder, and great love in his eyes, then lifted his hand slightly toward her. She knelt quickly and took it in both of hers, stroking it and kissing it.

"Oh, I ought to a'done better. I'm awful sorry I went back on Him. It was the lemonade. The boys didn't mean no harm."

Geordie hurled out some bitter words.

"Don't ye be too hard on 'em, Geordie," said Billy. "They meant no harm. Leave 'em to the hand o' the Almighty."

Then Mrs. Mavor began to sing *Just As I Am,* and Billy dozed off quietly for half an hour.

When he awoke again his eyes turned to Craig and they were troubled and anxious.

"I tried hard!" he said again. "I wanted to win." He was struggling with his speech. By this time Craig was master of himself, and he answered in a clear, distinct voice—

"Listen, Billy, you made a great fight, and you are going to win yet. And besides, do you remember the sheep that got lost over the mountains?"—the parable was one of Billy's favorites—"He didn't beat it when He got it back, did He? He took it in his arms and carried it home. And so He will you."

And keeping his eyes fastened on the minister, Billy said simply—

"Will He?"

"Sure will," answered Craig.

"Will He...really?" he repeated, turning his eyes upon Mrs. Mavor.

"Why yes, Billy," she answered cheerily, though the tears were streaming from her eyes. "I would, and He loves you even so much more, even than I do. And that must be a great deal."

He looked at her, smiled, and closed his eyes.

I put my hand on his heart. It was fluttering feebly. Again a troubled look passed over his face.

"My poor—old—mother," he whispered. "She's—she's in—in the—workhouse."

"I shall take care of her, Billy," said Mrs. Mavor, in a clear voice, and again Billy smiled. Then he turned his eyes to Craig, and from him to Geordie, and at last to Mrs. Mavor again, where they rested. She bent over and kissed him softly on the forehead.

"Tell her," he said with difficulty, "He's took me home."

"Yes, Billy," she answered, gazing into his glazing eyes.

He tried to lift her hand. She kissed him again. He drew in one last deep breath, then slowly exhaled, and his body lay still. He was gone to that new home for sheep, whose Shepherd has found them at last.

"Thank the blessed Saviour!" said Craig reverently. "He has taken him in His arms."

But Mrs. Mavor held the dead hand tight and sobbed out passionately. "Oh, Billy! Billy! You helped me once when I needed help badly. I will never forget you!"

Geordie groaned, "Ay, laddie, laddie!" and went out into the fading light of the early evening.

The next day no one went to work, for to one and all it seemed a sacred day. They carried Billy into the little church, and there Mr. Craig spoke of his long hard fight, and of his final victory. For he died without a fear, and with love to the men who, not knowing, had brought on his death.

And there was no bitterness in any heart, for Craig read the story of the sheep, and told how gently the Shepherd had taken Billy home. But though no official word was spoken, it was at Billy's funeral that the League was made again.

They laid him under the pine trees beside Lewis Mavor, and the miners threw sprigs of evergreen into the open grave. When Slavin, himself weeping over Billy's passing, brought his sprig, no one stopped him, though all thought it strange.

As we turned to leave the grave, the light from the evening sun came softly through the gap in the mountains and filled the valley and touched the trees and the little mound beneath with colorful glory.

And I thought of that other glory, which is brighter than the sun, and was not sorry that poor Billy's weary fight was over. I could not help but think that the forming of the League had been a good thing, and that more good was to come of it still.

15.
THE NEW LEAGUE

Billy Breen's legacy to the Black Rock mining camp was a new League, which was more than simply the old League put back together. The League was new in its spirit and in its methods.

The impression made upon the whole camp by Billy Breen's death was remarkable. I have never been quite able to account for it. It was truly one of those cases where the giving of a man's life propels a cause forward in a greater way than perhaps would have been possible otherwise.

The mood of the community at the time was peculiarly susceptible. Billy was one of the oldest of the old timers. His decline and fall had been a long process, and his struggle for life and manhood was striking enough to arrest the attention and awaken the sympathy of the whole camp. We instinctively side with a man in his struggle for freedom, for we fell that freedom is natural to him, and to us. Indeed, to all men and women.

Billy's sudden collapse stirred the men with a deep pity for his failure, and a deep contempt for those who had tricked him to his doom. But though the pity and the contempt remained, the gloom was relieved and the sense of defeat removed from the men's minds by the transforming glory of Billy's last hour. As Mr. Craig, telling of the tragedy of Billy's death, transformed defeat into victory, this became the generally accepted view of the thing, though to the men it was full of mystery. Yet they could all understand and appreciate at full value the spirit that breathed through the words of the dying man: "Don't be too hard on 'em. They didn't mean no harm."

This spirit of forgiveness became the new spirit of the League.

It was this spirit that surprised Slavin into sudden tears at the graveside. He had come all braced for curses and vengeance, and instead of vengeance the message from the dead that echoed through the voice of the living was one of pity and forgiveness.

The days of the League's negative, tooth-for-tooth, fight-fire-with-fire defensive warfare were thus over. The fight was to the death, and now the battle was to be carried into the enemy's country—into the very souls of the men of the Black Rock community. The war would henceforth be of a different kind altogether.

The new-League men proposed a thoroughly equipped and well-conducted coffee room, reading room, and hall, to parallel the enemy's lines of operation—open at the same time as Slavin's saloon, offering warmth and company and things to do at those very times when the men were weakest —and thus defeat them with their own weapons upon their own ground. The main outlines of the scheme were clearly defined and were easily seen, but the perfecting of the details called for all Craig's tact and good sense. He was still, after all, the general in charge of mustering his troops.

Entertainment was proposed. Shaw had charge of the social department, whose special care it was to see that the men were made welcome to the cozy, cheerful reading room, where they might chat, smoke, read, write letters, or play games, each according to his own fancy.

Craig felt that the success or failure of the scheme would largely depend upon the character of the Resident Manager, who, while caring for the reading room and hall, would control and operate the important department represented by the coffee room.

"We have to get the right man," he said one day to Mrs. Mavor, without whose counsel nothing was done. "Otherwise the whole thing will fall flat."

"We shall get the right man, never fear," she replied. Her serene courage never faltered. "He will come to us."

Craig turned to her with admiration. "If only I had your courage," he said.

"Courage!" she answered quickly. "It is not for you to say that." And at his answering look the red came into her cheek and the depths of her eyes glowed. And I wondered, looking at Craig's cool face, whether his blood was at that moment running evenly through his veins. But his voice was quiet, a shade too quiet I thought, as he gravely replied—

"I would often be a coward but for the shame of it."

And so the new League waited for the man to come who was to be Resident Manager and make the new enterprise a success. But I knew Mrs. Mavor and Jim Craig were not just waiting; they were praying for the right man to be sent.

Come he did, but the manner of his coming was so extraordinary that I could explain it in no way other than as an answer to their prayers. For as Craig said, "If he had come straight from Heaven, I could not have been more surprised."

While the League was thus waiting, its interest centered upon Slavin because he represented more than anyone else the forces of the enemy. Though the memory of Billy Breen stood between him and the vengeance of the angry men who would have made short work of him and his saloon—not *all* the League men were as forgiving as Billy might have wished; nothing could save him from himself. After the funeral

Slavin went to his bar and drank whisky as he had never drunk before. But the more he drank the fiercer and gloomier he became, and when the men drinking with him rankled him, he swore deeply and with such threats that they left him alone.

It did not help Slavin either to have Nixon stride in through the crowd drinking at his bar, accost him, and then give him words of warning.

"It is not by any of your doing, Slavin," he said in a slow, cool voice, "that you and your crew didn't send me to my death too the night of the ball. You won your bet. You got me back into the bottle. But I want to say that next time, though you are seven to one, or ten times that against me, that when any of you boys offer me drink I'll take you to a mean fight before I'll have it. Whatever Billy may have said about you meaning no harm, I don't believe it. And though the preacher says to forgive you, and though I'll do my best, I'll not drink. And I'll not disappoint you if it's a fight you want."

And so saying he strode out again, leaving a mean-looking crowd of men behind him. All who had not been involved in the business at Nixon's shack expressed approval of his position, and hoped he would see it through.

But the impression of Nixon's words upon Slavin was nothing compared with that made by Geordie Crawford. It was not so much what he said as the manner of awful solemnity his words carried. Geordie was struggling conscientiously to keep his promise not to be too hard on the boys. But his manner of "leavin' them in the hands o' the Almighty," was so grim that I could not but wonder that Slavin's superstitious Irish nature supplied him with supernatural terrors. It was the second day after the funeral that Geordie and I were walking toward Slavin's. There was a great shout of laughter as we drew near.

Geordie stopped short and said, "We'll jist go in a minute."

He walked through the swinging doors, passed through the crowd, and straight up to the bar.

"Michael Slavin," he said in a stern voice, and in an instant all the men in the place were staring at the confrontation in dead silence with their glasses in their hands. "Michael Slavin, I promised the lad I'd bear ye no ill will, but jist do my best to leave ye to the Almighty. An' I want to tell ye that I'm keepin' my word. But"—and here he raised his hand, and his voice became preternaturally solemn—"his blood is upon yer hands. Do ye not see it?"

His voice rose sharply, and as he pointed, Slavin instinctively glanced at his hands, and Geordie added—

"Ay, and the Lord will require it o' you and yer hoose!"

They told me that Slavin shivered as if taken with ague after Geordie went out, and though he laughed and swore, he did not stop drinking till he sank into a drunken stupor and had to be carried to bed. His little French-Canadian wife could not understand the change that had come over her husband.

"He's like one angry bear," she confided to Mrs. Mavor, to whom she was showing her one-year old baby. "He's not kiss me one time dis day. He's mos' awful bad, he's not even look at de baby." And this seemed sufficient proof that something was seriously wrong, for she went on—

"He's tink more for dat leel baby dan for de whole worl," and she shrugged her pretty little shoulders.

"You must pray for him," said Mrs. Mavor, "and all will come right."

"Ah," she replied earnestly, "every day I pray to all les saints for him."

"You must pray to your Father in heaven for him, not to the saints."

"Ah! Oui! I weel pray," and Mrs. Mavor sent her away bright with smiles, and with new hope and courage in her heart.

144

She very soon had need of all her courage, for at the week's end her baby fell dangerously ill. Slavin's anxiety and fear were not relieved much by the reports the men brought him from time to time of Geordie's ominous forebodings. For Geordie had no doubt but that the Avenger of Blood was hot upon Slavin's trail. And as the sickness grew, he became confirmed in this conviction. While he could not be said to find satisfaction in Slavin's impending affliction, he could hardly hide his complacency in the promptness of Providence in vindicating his theory of retribution.

But Geordie's complacency was somewhat rudely shocked by Craig's answer to his theory one day.

"You read your Bible to little profit, it seems to me, Geordie," the minister said, "or perhaps you have never read the Master's teaching about the Tower of Siloam. Better read that and take that warning to yourself."

Geordie gazed after Craig as he turned away, then muttered—

"The toor o' Siloam, is it? Ay, I ken fine aboot the toor o' Siloam, and aboot the toor o' Babel as weel. And I've read too about the blaspheemious Herod, and such like. Man, but he's a hot-headed laddie, and lacks discreemeenation."

"What about Herod?" I asked.

"Aboot Herod?" he repeated, with a strong tinge of contempt in his tone. "Aboot Herod, ye say? Man, hae ye no read in the Screepturs aboot Herod and the worms in the stomach o' him?"

"Oh yes, I see," I hastened to answer.

"A fule can aye see what's flapped in his face." And with that bit of proverbial philosophy he suddenly left me. But Geordie thenceforth contented himself, in Craig's presence at least, with ominous head-shakings, equally aggravating and impossible to answer.

That same night, however, Geordie showed that with all his theories he had a man's true heart, for he came in haste to Mrs. Mavor's.

"Ye'll be needed over yonder, I'm thinkin'," he said.

"Why, is the baby worse?" she asked in alarm. "Have you been inside?"

"Na, na," replied Geordie cautiously. "I'll no go where I'm no wanted. But you poor thing, ye can hear outside the weepin' and moanin'."

Mrs. Mavor wasted no time in gathering her few needful items and hastening out the door to Slavin's.

"She'll maybe need ye as weel," Geordie went on dubiously to me. "Ye're a kind o' doctor, I hear," not committing himself to any opinion as to my professional value.

I went, but Slavin would have none of me. Somehow he managed to get the doctor sober enough to prescribe something.

16.
WHAT CAME TO SLAVIN

The interest of the whole town in Slavin was greatly increased by the illness of his baby, which was the apple of his eye. There were a few who, impressed by Geordie's profound convictions upon the matter, were inclined to favor the retribution theory and connect the baby's illness with the vengeance of the Almighty. Among these few was Slavin himself, and goaded by his remorseful terrors and guilt, he sought relief in drink. But this brought him only deeper and deeper into his gloom, so that between her suffering child and her savagely despairing and guilt-ridden husband, the poor mother was beside herself with grief.

"My heart is broken for him," she sobbed to Mrs. Mavor. "He's eat noting for tree days, but jis dreenk, dreenk, dreenk."

The next day a man came for me in haste. The baby was dying and the doctor was drunk.

I ran to the house and found the little one in a convulsion, lying across Mrs. Mavor's knees, the mother kneeling beside it, wringing her hands, and Slavin standing nearby, silent and suffering inwardly. I glanced at the bottle of med-

147

icine on the table and asked Mrs. Mavor what dosage had been given. The answer told me nothing less than that the baby had been poisoned. The sudden look of horror on my face said immediately to Slavin that something was seriously wrong. Striding to me he caught my arm and asked—

"What is it? Is the medicine wrong?"

I tried to evade the question, but his grip tightened till his fingers seemed to reach the bone.

"The dose was certainly too large, but let me go, I must see if I can do something."

He let me go at once, saying in a voice that made my heart sore for him, "He has killed my baby. He has killed my baby." And then he began to curse the doctor with awful oaths, and with a look of such murderous fury on his face that I was glad the doctor was too drunk to make an appearance.

Hearing his angry voice, and understanding the cause, his wife broke out into wailing.

"Ah! Mon petit angel! It's dat wheeskey dat's keel my baby. Ah, mon cheri, mon amour. Ah, mon Dieu! Ah, Michael, how often I tell you dat wheeskey be not a good ting."

Her stinging words were more than Slavin could bear, and with awful curses he left the room. Mrs. Mavor laid the baby in its crib, for the convulsion had passed. She put her arms around the wailing little Frenchwoman, comforting and soothing her as a mother might her child.

"You must help your husband," I heard her say. "He will need you more than ever. Think of him."

"Ah, oui! I weel," came the reply.

It seemed hardly more than a minute till Slavin came in again, sober, quiet, and steady. The passion was all gone from his face. Only the grief remained.

As we stood leaning over the sleeping child the little thing opened its eyes, saw its father, and smiled. It was too much for him. The big man dropped on his knees with a dry sob.

"Is there no chance at all?" he whispered. But I could give him no hope. What I knew of modern medicine was very little, and I knew nothing for this. Had we been in Toronto, perhaps. But in Black Rock, what could be done? Slavin immediately rose, pulled himself together, and stood perfectly quiet.

Suddenly a new terror seized upon the mother.

"My baby is not—what you call it?" and she made the motions to indicate baptism.

"Do not fear for your little one," said Mrs. Mavor, still with her arms about her. "The good Saviour will take your darling into His own arms."

But the mother would not be comforted by this. And Slavin too was uneasy.

"Where is Father Goulet?" he asked.

"You were not good to the holy pere de las time, Michael," she replied sadly. "The saints are not pleased with you."

"Where is the priest?" he demanded.

"I know not for sure. At de Landin' perhaps."

"I'll go for him," he said. But his wife clung to him, begging him not to leave.

I left, found Craig, and told him the difficulty. With his usual promptness, he was ready with a solution.

"Nixon has a team. He will go."

Then he added, "I wonder if they would like me to baptize the little one. Father Goulet and I have exchanged offices a few times in the past. I remember how he came to one of my people in my absence, when she was dying, read with her, prayed with her, comforted her, and helped her across the river. He is a good soul, and has no nonsense about him. Send for me if you think they would have me. It will make no difference to the baby, but it will comfort the mother."

Nixon was willing enough to go, but when he came to the Slavin's door, Mrs. Mavor saw the hard look on his face.

He had still not forgotten Slavin's hand in his downfall. But Mrs. Mavor, under cover of getting him instructions, drew him into the room.

"They fear the little one will never see the Saviour if it is not baptised," she said in a low tone.

In an instant, with one look at the little white face in the crib, Nixon's resentments were gone.

I'll do my best to get the priest," he said, and was gone on his sixty mile race with death.

The long afternoon wore on, but before it was half gone I saw that Nixon could not win and that the priest would be too late. I sent for Craig. From the moment he entered the room he took command. He was so simple, so manly, so tender, the hearts of the two despondent parents instinctively turned to him.

As he was about to proceed with the baptism, the mother whispered to Mrs. Mavor, who then, with some hesitation in her voice, asked Craig if he would object to using holy water.

"To me it is as good as any other," he replied.

"And will he make the good sign?" asked the mother timidly.

Thus the child was baptised by the Presbyterian minister with holy water and with the sign of the cross. I don't suppose it was orthodox by either Presbyterian or Catholic or any other standards, and it rendered chaotic some of my religious notions. But I thought more of Craig in that moment than ever before. He was more a man than a minister, or perhaps he was so good a minister because so gracious and compassionate a man. As he read about the Saviour and the children and the disciples who tried to get in between them, and as he told us the story in his own simple and beautiful way, and then went on to picture the home of the little children, and the same Saviour in the midst of them, I felt my heart grow warm, and I could easily understand the cry of the mother—

"Oh, mon Jesu, prenez moi aussi, take me with my baby."

The cry wakened Slavin's heart, and he said huskily—

"Oh, Annette!"

"Oui, and Michael too!" she cried. Then to Craig—

"You think He's tak me someday?"

"All who love him," he replied.

"And Michael too?" she asked, her eyes searching his face. "And my Michael too?"

But Craig only replied, "All who love him."

"Oh, Michael, you must pray to le bon Jesu. He's garde notre mignon."

And then she bent over the baby, whispering—

"Ah, mon cheri, adieu! Adieu, mon angel!" till Slavin put his arms about her and took her away. As she was whispering her farewells, with a little answering sigh, her baby passed into the House with many rooms.

"Don't cry, Annette, darlin'. Don't cry for the baby," said her husband. "It's sure better off than the rest of us. An' didn't ye hear what the minister said about the beautiful place he is in? An' he sure wouldn't lie to us." But the mother could not be comforted for her first-born son.

An hour later Nixon brought Father Goulet. He was a little Frenchman with gentle manners and the face of a saint. Craig welcomed him warmly, and told him what he had done.

"That is good, my brother," he said, with gentle courtesy. Then turning to the mother, "Your little one is safe."

Behind Father Goulet came Nixon softly, and gazed down upon the little quiet face, beautiful with the magic of death. Slavin came quietly and stood beside him. Nixon turned, offered his hand, and said, "I'm sorry, Slavin."

But Slavin moved slowly back, saying—

"I did ye a wrong, Nixon, and I'm the one that's sorry for it this day."

"Don't say a word about it," answered Nixon hurriedly.

"I know how you feel. I've got a baby too. I want to see it again. That's why the break hurt me so."

"As God's above," replied Slavin earnestly, "I'll hinder ye no more."

They shook hands, and we left the house.

We laid the baby under the pines, not far from Billy Breen, and the sweet spring wind blew through the Gap and came softly down the valley, whispering to the pines and the grass and the hiding flowers of the New Life coming to the world. The mother must have heard the whisper in her heart, for as the Priest was saying the words of the Service she stood with Mrs. Mavor's arms about her, and her eyes were looking far away beyond the purple mountain-tops, seeing what made her smile. And Slavin too looked different. His very features seemed finer. The coarseness was gone out of his face. What had come to him I could not tell.

But when the doctor came into Slavin's house that night it was the old Slavin I saw, with a look of such deadly fury on his face that I tried to get the doctor out at once. But he was half drunk and after his manner attempted to be what could only be described as hideously humorous.

"How do, ladies! How do, gentlemen!" was his loud-voiced salutation. "Quite a professional gathering, clergy predominating. Lion and Lamb too, Ha! Ha! Which is the lamb, eh? Ha! Ha! Very good! Awfully sorry to hear of your loss, Mrs. Slavin. Did our best you know, can't help this sort of thing."

Before anyone could move, Craig was at his side, and saying in a clear, firm voice, "One moment, doctor," caught him by the arm and had him out of the house before he knew it.

Slavin had been crouching in his chair with hands twitching and eyes glaring, and now he rose and followed, still crouching as he walked. I hurried after him, calling him back. Turning at my voice, the doctor saw Slavin approaching. There was something so terrifying in his swift noiseless

152

crouching motion, that the doctor, crying out in fear, "Keep him off me," fairly turned and fled.

He was too late. Like a tiger Slavin leaped upon him and without waiting to strike had him by the throat with both hands, and throwing him to the ground, fell upon him.

Immediately Craig and I were upon him, but though we lifted him clear off the ground we could not loosen that two-handed strangling grip. As we were struggling a light hand touched my shoulder. It was Father Goulet.

"Please let him go, and stand away from us," he said, waving us back.

We obeyed.

He leaned over Slavin and spoke a few words to him. Slavin started as if struck by a heavy blow, looked up at the priest with fear in his face, but still kept his grip.

"Let him go," said the priest.

Still Slavin hesitated.

"Let him go, quick!" said the priest again, and with a snarl Slavin let go his hold and stood sullenly facing the priest.

Father Goulet regarded him steadily for some seconds, and then asked—

"What would you do?" His voice was gentle enough, even sweet, but there was something in it that chilled my bones to the marrow. "What would you do?" he repeated.

"He murdered my child," growled Slavin.

"And how was that?"

"He was drunk and poisoned him."

"And who gave him the drink?"

Slavin stood still and did not answer.

"Who made him a drunkard two years ago? Who gave him the drink that wrecked his life?"

Still there was no answer. And the even-toned voice went relentlessly on—

"Who is the murderer of your child now?"

Slavin groaned and shuddered.

"Go!" and the voice grew stern. "Repent of your sin and add not another upon it."

Slavin turned his eyes upon the motionless figure on the ground and then upon the priest. Father Goulet took one step toward him, and, stretching out his hand and pointing with his finger, said again—

"Go!"

Slowly Slavin backed away and went into his house.

It was an extraordinary scene, and it has remained with me all these years: the dark figure on the ground, the slight erect form of the priest with outstretched arm and finger, and Slavin backing away, fear and fury and guilt all struggling upon his face.

It was a near thing for the doctor, however. His body was in a considerably weakened state by the alcohol already, and two minutes more of that grip would have done him in. As it was, we had the greatest difficulty in reviving him. But eventually he began to come to his senses with a low groan.

What the priest did with Slavin after getting him inside I do not know. That has always remained a mystery to me. But it was clearly a conversation which had the most profound impact upon Slavin, for from that moment on he was a different man.

When we were passing the saloon that night after taking Mrs. Mavor home, we saw a light and heard strange sounds inside. Entering, we found another whisky raid in progress. But this time it was Slavin himself who was the raider. We stood some moments watching him knocking in the heads of casks and emptying bottles. I thought he may have gone mad, and approached him cautiously.

"Hello, Slavin," I called out, "what does this mean?"

He paused in his strange work, and I saw that his face, though resolute, was quiet enough.

"It means I'm done with the business, I am," he said in

a determined voice. "I'll help no more to kill any man, or," in a lower tone, "any man's baby." The priest's words had struck home.

"Thank God, Slavin!" said Craig, approaching and offering his hand warmly, "you are much too good a man for this business!"

"Good or bad, I'm done with it," he replied, going on with his work.

"You are throwing away good money, Slavin," I said, as the head of a cask crashed in.

"It's myself that knows it, for the price of whisky has gone up considerable this week," he answered, giving me a look out of the corner of his eye. "It was a rare clever job," referring to our Black Rock Hotel affair.

"But won't you be sorry for this?" asked Craig.

"No doubt I will, an' that's why I'm doin' it now before I has the chance to be sorry for it," he replied, with a delightful swing of a hammer against a new barrel.

"Look here, Slavin," said Craig earnestly, "if I can be of use to you in any way, count on me."

"It's good to me the both of you have been, an' I'll not forget it to you," he replied with like earnestness.

As we told Mrs. Mavor that night, for Craig thought it too good to keep to ourselves, her eyes seemed to grow deeper and the light in them to glow more intense as she listened to Craig pouring out his tale. Then she gave him her hand and said—

"So, you have your man at last."

"What man?"

"The man you have been waiting and praying for."

"Slavin!"

"Why not?"

"I never thought of it."

"No more did he, nor any of us." Then after a pause, she added gently, "God has sent him to us."

"Do you know, I believe you are right," Craig said slowly, and then added, "But you always are."

"I fear that is hardly true," she answered, but I could tell she liked to hear the words, coming from him.

The whole town was astounded the next morning when Slavin went to work in the mines. The doors of his saloon remained locked the entire day and into the evening. The astonishment only deepened as the days went on, and he stuck to his work and the doors to the saloon remained shut.

Before three weeks had passed, the League had bought and begun to remodel the saloon, and had secured Slavin as Resident Manager.

The evening of the reopening of Slavin's saloon, as it was still called, was long remembered in Black Rock. It was the occasion of the first appearance of "The League Minstrel and Dramatic Troupe," in what was described as a "hair-lifting tragedy with appropriate musical selections."

Then followed a grand supper and speeches and great enthusiasm, which reached its climax when Nixon rose to propose the toast of the evening—"*Our* Saloon." His speech was simply a quiet, manly account of his long struggle with the deadly enemy. When he came to speak of his recent defeat he said—

"And while I am blaming no one but myself, I am glad tonight that this saloon is on our side, for my own sake and for the sake of those who have been waiting long to see me back home. But before I sit down I want to say that while I live I shall not forget that I owe my life to the man that took me that night to his own cabin and put me in his own bed, and met me the next morning with an open hand of love. For I tell you I had sworn to God that that morning would be my last."

Geordie's speech was characteristic. After a brief reference to the "mysteerious ways o' Providence," which he acknowledged he might sometimes fail to understand, he went on to express his unqualified approval of the new saloon.

"It's a cozy place, an' there's nae sulphur aboot. Besides that," he went on enthusiastically, "it'll be a terrible savin' for us all. I've jist been coontin'."

"You bet!" added a voice with great emphasis.

"I've jist been coontin'," repeated Geordie, ignoring the remark and the laughter which followed it, "an' it's an awful sum o' money ye all put into the whisky. Ye canna do wi' jist one wee glass; ye must have two or three at the very least, an' before ye ken what's come ower ye, ye've spent yer whole paycheck. But wi' coffee, ye jist get a sixpence worth an' ye want nae more."

There was another shout of laughter, which puzzled Geordie.

"I dinna see the joke, but I've slipped ower whisky mysel' for more'n a hunner dollars. But since I quit, I'm savin' it up again."

Then he paused, looking hard before him, and twisting his face into extraordinary shapes till the men looked at him curiously.

"I'm real glad o' this saloon," he went on, his voice soft and shaky, "but it's too late for the lad that canna be helped nae more noo. He'll not be needin' oor kind o' help, I dinna doobt. But there are others"—and he stopped abruptly and sat down, with no applause following.

But when Slavin, former saloon keeper for whisky and now saloon keeper for the coffee house, rose to reply, the men jumped up on the seats and yelled till they could yell no more. Slavin stood, evidently in timid embarrassment over their wholehearted acceptance of the League's former enemy, and then finally broke out—

"I'm speechless entirely! What's to come to me I don't know yet. I don't hardly know how it's come. But I'll do my best for the lot o' you!" And the yelling broke out again.

I did not enter into the hoopla myself. I was too busy watching the varying lights in Mrs. Mavor's eyes as she looked from Craig to the cheering men on the benches and tables, and then to Slavin.

I found myself wondering if she knew more deeply than I just what it was that came to Slavin that so changed his heart.

17.
THE TWO CALLS

With the call to Mr. Craig I fancy I had something to do myself. I was foolish enough at the time to think I was helping him toward a greater work than he was now doing. As if anything could be greater than what he had accomplished.

The call came from a young congregation in an Eastern city, and was based partly upon his college record and more upon the advice of those among the authorities who knew his work in the mountains. No doubt my letters to friends who were of importance in that congregation were not without influence, for I was then of the mind that the man who could handle Black Rock miners as he could was ready for something larger than a mountain mission.

I had not for a moment imagined that he would refuse, though by then I ought to have known him better. He was but little troubled over it. He went with the offer of the pulpit and the letters urging his acceptance to Mrs. Mavor, in the back of whose house I had set up a little studio. I was just putting the last touches to some of my work when he came to call on her. I came out with her, not realizing what was to come.

She read the letters and the invitation of the position very quietly, and then waited for him to speak.

"Well?" he said. "Should I go?"

She grew a little pale. His question suggested a possibility that had not occurred to her. That he could leave his work in Black Rock she had never imagined. I saw the fear in her face, but I saw more than fear in her eyes, as for a moment or two she let them rest upon Craig's face. For the first time I began to have a sense of regret over what I may have done. But she was too much a woman to show her heart easily to the man she loved, and her voice was even and calm as she answered his question.

"Is this a very large congregation?"

"One of the finest in the East," I put in for him. "It will be a great stride forward for Craig."

Craig was studying her curiously. I think she noticed his eyes upon her, for she went on even more quietly—

"It will be a great chance for work, and you are well qualified for a larger sphere of influence, you know, than poor Black Rock affords."

"Who will take Black Rock?" he asked.

"Let some other fellow have a try at it," I said. "Why should you waste your talents here?"

"Waste!" cried Mrs. Mavor indignantly.

"Well, *bury* if you like it better," I replied.

"It would not take much of a grave for that funeral," said Craig, smiling.

"Oh," said Mrs. Mavor, "you will be a great man, I know, and perhaps you ought to go now."

But he answered coolly, "There are fifty men wanting that Eastern pulpit, and there is only one wanting the humble little church of Black Rock. And I don't think Black Rock is anxious for a change. So I think I will stay where I am yet a while."

I could see the sudden leap of joy in Mrs. Mavor's eyes, but with a great effort, she answered quietly—

"Black Rock will be very glad, and some of us very, very glad."

Nothing could change his mind. I tried half-heartedly a time or two, for the truth had still not entirely dawned on me. There was no one he knew who could take his place just now, and even if there had been, why should he quit his work? What was a fancy Eastern congregation to him?

If any further doubts about the matter remained in my own mind, the next Sabbath evening would have removed them. For during the service he shared briefly the decision he had had to make, and afterward the men all came about him and let him know in their own way how much they approved his decision. Though the self-sacrifice involved did not impress them much. They were too truly Western to imagine that any inducements the East could offer could compensate for his loss of the West. It was only fitting that the West should have the best, and so the miners took it almost as a matter of course, and certainly as their right, that the best man they knew should stay with them. But there were those who knew how much of what most men consider worth-while he had given up, and they loved him all the more for it.

The call which came to Mrs. Mavor was not so easily disposed of. It came but one week after Craig's, and stirred Black Rock as nothing else had ever stirred it before.

I found her one afternoon gazing vacantly at some legal documents spread out before her on the table, evidently overcome by their contents. There was first a lawyer's letter informing her that by the death of her husband's father she had come into the whole of the Mavor estates and all the wealth pertaining thereto. The letter asked for instructions, and urged her immediate return with a view to her own personal superintendence of the estates. Another letter, from a distant cousin of her husband, urged her immediate return for many reasons, but chiefly on account of the old mother who had been left alone with no one nearer of kin than himself to care for her in her old age.

With these two came another letter from her mother-in-law herself. The shaky letters were even more eloquent than the words with which the letter closed.

"I have lost my boy, and now my husband is gone, and I am a lonely woman. I have many servants, and some dear friends, but none near to me, none so near and dear as my dead son's wife. My days are not to be many. Come to me, my daughter. I want you and Lewis's child."

"Must I go?" she asked with white lips.

"Do you know her well?" I asked.

"I only saw her once or twice," she answered. "But she has been very good to me."

"She must have friends to see to her. And surely you are needed here."

She looked at me eagerly.

"Do you really think so?" she said.

"Ask any man in the camp—Shaw, Nixon, young Winton, Geordie. Ask Craig," I replied.

"Yes, he will tell me," she said, and the light was in her eyes again as she spoke.

18.
AN AGONIZING DECISION

Even as Mrs. Mavor and I were speaking, Craig came up the steps. I went back into my studio and proceeded with my work, for my days at Black Rock were coming to an end and many sketches remained to be filled in. Instinctively I knew what was coming between the two of them, and I closed the door. But I could hardly keep from hearing snatches of what was said. And many details were filled in to me later, for I had grown very close to each of them, and they readily confided in me.

Mrs. Mavor laid her letters before Mr. Craig, saying, "The East is calling me too."

He went through the papers, then carefully laid them down without a word while she waited anxiously, almost impatiently, for him to speak.

"Well?" she asked, using his own words to her, "should I go?"

"I do not know," he replied. "That is for you to decide —you know all the circumstances."

"The letters tell everything." Her tone carried a feeling of disappointment. He did not appear to care.

163

"The estates are large?" he asked.

"Yes, large enough—twelve thousand a year."

"Has your mother-in-law anyone with her?"

"She has friends, but, as she says, none near of kin. Her nephew looks after the works—iron works, you know—he shares in them."

"She is evidently very lonely," he answered.

"What shall I do?" she asked. It was clear she was waiting, hoping against hope that he would urge her to stay. But Craig was trying so hard to quiet his own heart's pain at the thought of her leaving, that he was momentarily blind to *her* heart, which had placed its future in his hands.

"I cannot say," he repeated quietly, hardly thinking of his words. His mind was spinning. He desperately wanted to shout out *Stay! I love you. Remain here with me!* But he feared her response. "There are many things to consider," he finally went on, "the estates, those who are depending upon you—"

"The estates seem to trouble you," she replied almost fretfully.

He looked up in surprise. Still he did not perceive the look in her eyes.

"Yes...yes, the estates," he went on, "and tenants, I suppose—and your mother-in-law, your little Marjorie's future, your own future. No doubt there is far more for you there than to remain in this backward place."

"Everything is in capable hands," she replied, "and my future depends—"

Here she hesitated, and then quickly resumed.

"—my future depends upon what I choose my work to be."

"But when responsibilities are thrust upon you—"

"I do not want them!" she cried.

"That sort of life has great opportunities for doing good," he said kindly, still thinking he was urging her toward what she wanted.

"I had thought that perhaps there was work for me here," she suggested timidly.

"Great work," he hastened to say, his heart giving a flutter at the very possibility that she might *stay*! The most obvious solution he had never stopped to consider. "You have done great work here! And you will wherever you go." Then he added, "The only question is where your work lies."

"You think I should go," she said suddenly, her voice growing a little bitter in its disappointment.

"I cannot bid you stay," he answered steadily. "That would not be right of me, to stand in the way of—"

"How can I go?" she cried, appealing to him. "My work is here. My heart is here. How can I go? You thought it worth your while to stay here and work. Why should I not?"

She glanced away. She could not look into his eyes again.

A momentary gleam came into his eye. At last the truth began slowly to dawn on his stubborn man's heart.

"I know you do not need me," she went on in the intensity of her feeling. "You have your work, your miners, your plans. You need no one. You are strong. But," and her voice rose to a cry, "I am not strong by myself. You have made me strong, I came here a foolish girl, foolish and selfish and narrow. God sent me grief. Three years ago my heart died. Now I am living again. I am a woman now, no longer a girl. You have done this for me. Your life, your words, yourself—you have shown me a better life, a higher life, than I had ever known before, and now you would send me away."

She paused abruptly.

"Have I done this for you?" he said slowly, disbelievingly. "Then surely God had been good to me. For you have helped me more than any words could tell you."

"Helped!" she repeated.

"Yes, helped," he answered.

"You can do without my help," she went on. "You make people help you. You will get many to help you. But I need help too."

She was standing before him with her hands tightly clasped. Her face was pale and her eyes deeper than ever. He stood looking at her in a kind of daze as she poured out her words hot and fast.

"I have grown to depend upon you, to look to you. What shall I do alone? It is nothing to you that I go, but to me—"

She did not dare finish.

Craig slowly approached and stood before her, his face deadly pale.

"Ah, if only you knew," he said. His voice was tender and quiet. "You do not guess what you are doing to my heart."

"What am I doing? What is there to know but that you tell me I should go?" She was struggling with the tears she was too proud to let him see.

He had been standing with his hands resolutely behind him, looking at her as if studying her face for the first time. Under his searching look she dropped her eyes, and the warm color came slowly up into her neck and face. Then, as if with a sudden resolve, she lifted her eyes to his, and looked back at him without flinching.

He started, surprised, and drew slowly near. The look of love in her eyes told all. At last he perceived the truth. Slowly he reached forward and took her two hands in his. She never moved her eyes, and they drew him toward her. He dropped her hands and caressed her cheek, smiled into her eyes, then kissed her lips tenderly.

She put her head upon his breast and reached her arms about him. Thus they stood in silent bliss for several moments.

After a minute Craig stepped back, took her hands

again, looked her full in the face, and said—

"No, you shall not go. I shall never let you go."

She gave a little contented sigh, then smiled up at him and said—

"I *can* go now...or stay. I will be happy wherever I am, just knowing that you love me."

"Ah, my darling Mrs. Mavor," said Craig, "nothing shall take you away from me now. We shall work here together."

"If only we might," she said. "My heart could desire nothing more. "But what if you are right, that I must see to my other responsibilities?"

"Do we not love one another?" was his answer.

"Yes! Yes, of course," she said, "but sometimes love is not all."

"But love is the best."

"Yes," she said sadly, "love is the best. And it is for love's sake we will do the best."

"There is no better work than here. Surely this is best," and he pictured his plans for Black Rock before her. She listened eagerly.

"Oh! If it should be right," she cried, "my heart longs for nothing more. But I know you too well. I know that eventually, when your heart stills, though you may love me more than ever, you will consider the needs of others, even above our own happiness. You can do no other, Jim Craig, and that is why I love you. I fear for what you will tell me I must do. But I will do what you say. You are good, you are wise, and you shall tell me. For I know you love me."

He stood silent some moments, then burst out passionately—

"Why then has love come to us? We did not seek it. Surely love is of God. Does God mock us?"

He threw himself into a chair, pouring out his words of passionate protestation. She listened, smiling, then came to him and, touching his hair as a mother might her child's, said—

"You will be shown what is right, I have no fear of that. And what more could we wish to do but what is right. God will show you."

He stood up, took both her hands, looked long into her eyes, then turned abruptly away and went out.

She stood where he left her for some moments, her face radiant and her hands pressed upon her heart. Then she came toward my room. She found me busy with my painting, but as I looked up and met her eyes, she flushed slightly, and said—

"I quite forgot you."

"So it appeared."

"You heard?"

"Only pieces. I would have left the house, but it would have been rude to interrupt."

"Well, I am glad you know."

"I have known for sometime."

"How could you? I only knew today myself."

"I have eyes," I said.

She flushed again.

"Do you mean that people—" she began anxiously.

"No, not *people*. I only said that *I* have eyes, and that they have been opened to how things stood between yourself and Craig."

"Opened?"

"Yes, by love."

Then I told her how, weeks ago, I had had to struggle with my own heart, and mastered it. I saw it was vain to love her, because she loved a better man who loved her in return. She looked at me shyly and said—

"I am sorry."

"Don't worry," I replied cheerfully. "I didn't break my heart. I managed to stop it in time."

"I fear he will tell me that I must go back East," she said suddenly.

"I hope he is no such fool," I replied, hardly thinking

168

what I was about.

"Please, Mr. Connor," she said, "do not speak of him so. Do you think he would send me away if it were not for the best? He is the most selfless man I know. And I must trust that his selflessness extends to me also, and is always looking for my best too."

I must confess I was grieved with the very possibility of separation for these two, to whom love meant so much. Love for a woman like this comes only once to a man, and then he carries it with him through the length of his life, and warms his heart with it in death. So my heart could not help but be sore as I sat looking up at this woman who stood before me, overflowing with the joy of her new love, and dully conscious of the coming pain. But I soon found it was futile to urge my opinion that she should remain and share the work and life of the man she loved. She was already in a higher sphere. She only answered—

"You will help him all you can? For it will hurt him to have me go."

The quiver in her voice took out of my heart all the annoyance toward Craig, and I readily pledged myself to do what I could to help him.

It was later that night when I came upon him in his cabin, sitting in the light of his fire. I could instantly tell that he must be let alone. Some battles we fight side by side, with comrades cheering us and being cheered to victory. But there are fights we may not share, and these are deadly fights where lives are won and lost. So I could only lay my hand upon his shoulder without a word. He looked up quickly, read my face, and said with a groan—

"You know?"

I nodded.

"I fear she will want to go," he said despairingly.

"Then you must tell her to stay," I replied.

"But I am not sure that is the right path. God only knows. I cannot see it all clearly yet. But the light will come."

"May I tell you how I see it?" I asked.

"Go on," he said.

For the next twenty minutes I talked, passionately I fear, urging the reasons upon him for their both remaining in Black Rock together. Now I had completely reversed my position that only a week ago would have had him accepting a prestigious Eastern church. Vehemently I said that she would be doing no more than before, no more than is the common role of every woman. Her mother-in-law had a comfortable home, all that wealth could procure, good servants, and friends. The estates could be managed well enough without her. After a few years' work here they could go East for little Marjorie's education. Why should two lives be broken?—and so I went on. But still I failed to see the larger picture.

He listened carefully, even eagerly.

"You make a good case," he said with a slight smile. "But it is not a matter of the advantages on one side or the other. It is a matter of what God wants, of what is best in *His* plan. And that is something we can often not perceive. I will take a little time. Perhaps you are right. The light will come. Surely it will come. The Lord will reveal His will. But," and here he lifted his hands full length above his head, "I am not sorry. Whatever comes I am not sorry. It is great to have her love, but greater to love her as I do. Thank God! Nothing can take that away. I am willing, even glad to suffer for the joy of loving her."

The next morning, before I was awake, he was gone. There was a note waiting for me:—

> *"MY DEAR CONNOR,—I am due at the Landing. When I see you again I have no doubt the way will be clear. I will pray fervently as I go. Now all is dark. But He will show me His will. At times I am such a coward, and often, as you sometimes kindly inform me, a donkey, but I hope I never become a mule.*

"I am willing to be led, or want to be, at any rate. I must do the best—not second best—for her, for me, for her family in the East. The best only is God's will. What else would you have? Be good to her these days while I am gone, dear old fellow. —Yours,

Craig."

How often those words have braced me he will never know. I am a better man for them. "The best only is God's will. What else would you have?"

I determined then and there as I put the note down that I would fret no more, and that I would bother neither of them with argument nor expostulation. The decision had to be theirs alone. My only responsibility at present, as my friend had asked, was to "be good to her."

19.
LOVE IS NOT ALL

Those days when we were awaiting Craig's return, we spent many peaceful hours in the woods or on the mountainsides, or in the canyon beside the stream that danced down to meet the Black Rock River. I talked and sketched and read, Mrs. Mavor listened and dreamed, often with a happy smile upon her face. But there were moments when a cloud of fear would sweep the smile away, and then I would talk of Craig till the smile came back again.

The woods and the mountains and the river were her best, her wisest friends during those days. How sweet was the ministry of the woods to her. The trees were in their new summer leaves, fresh and full of life. They swayed and rustled above us, and their swaying and rustling soothed and comforted like the voice and touch of a mother. And the mountains, too, in all the glory of their varying robes of blues and purples, stood calmly, solemnly about us, uplifting our souls into regions of rest. The changing lights and shadows flitted swiftly over their rugged fronts, but left them ever as before in their steadfast majesty. And ever the little river sang of its cheerful courage, fearing not the great mountains that threatened to bar its passage to the sea. Mrs. Mavor heard the song and her courage rose also.

But through these days I sometimes felt I could not understand her, and I found myself studying her as I might a new acquaintance. Years had fallen from her. She was a girl again, full of young warm life. She was as sweet as before, but there was soft shyness over her, a half-shamed, half-frank consciousness in her face, a glad light in her eyes that made her all new to me. Her perfect trust in Craig was touching to see.

"He will tell me what to do," she would say, till I began to realize how impossible it would be for him to betray such trust, and be anything but true to the best.

I found myself dreading Craig's homecoming so much that I sent for Graeme and old man Nelson, who was more and more Graeme's trusted counselor and friend. They were both highly excited by the story I shared, for I thought it best to tell them everything.

"Craig will know better than any of us what is right to do," said Graeme when I was done, "and he will do that. No man can turn him from it. And," he added, "I should be sorry to try."

"But they love each other," I cried. "It would be a tremendous shame for them to part. What you are saying is sentimental humbug."

"Come on, Connor," urged Graeme. "Don't work yourself up over it. It's useless. Craig will walk his own way where his light falls. We're not going to change his mind whatever we do. And for my part, I would not have him be other than who he is. For if he weakens like the rest of us, the North Star will have dropped from my sky."

I muttered something stupid in reply.

When Craig rode up one morning after a little more than a week had passed, his face told me he had fought his fight and had not been beaten. He had ridden all night and was ready to drop with weariness.

"Connor, old boy," he said, putting out his hand, "I'm played out. There was a bad row at the Landing. I have just closed poor Colley's eyes. It was awful. I must get some sleep. Look after Dandy, will you?"

I shook his hand and nodded, hoping for some word other than instructions about his horse. But in that I was frustrated.

"Wake me in the afternoon," he said. "Perhaps you will go and tell her"—his lips quivered—"tell her I am back, but just now my nerve is gone." Then with a very wan smile, he added, "I am giving you a lot of trouble."

"Go to thunder!" I burst out. "It's no trouble. Of course I'll do it."

"I think I'd rather go to sleep," he replied, still smiling. I could hardly speak, and was glad of the chance to be alone with Dandy.

When I came in a little later I found him sitting with his head in his arms upon the table, fast asleep. I made tea, woke him up, forced him to take a warm bath, and sent him to bed. Then I went to Mrs. Mavor. I went with a fearful heart, but that was because I had forgotten the kind of woman she was.

She was standing in the light of the window waiting for me. Her face was pale but steady, there was a proud light in her fathomless eyes, a slight smile parted her lips, and she carried her head like a queen.

"Come in," she said. "You need not fear to tell me. I saw him ride home. I am proud of him. I know he loves me. And I know he will be true."

She drew in her breath sharply, and a faint color tinged her cheek. "But," she went on, "he knows love is not all! It is so painful, but I am glad and proud."

"Glad!" I gasped.

"You would not have him prove faithless?"

"That is all just sentimental nonsense," I could not help saying.

"Honor, faith, and duty are sentiments," she answered. "But they are not nonsense."

In spite of my annoyance I was lost in admiration for the high spirit of the woman who stood up so straight before me. When I told her how worn and tired he was, she listened with changing color and swelling heart, her proud courage giving way to love, anxious and pitying.

"Shall I go to him?" she asked with timid eagerness.

"He is sleeping," I replied. "He said he would come to you."

"I shall wait for him," she said softly. The tenderness in her tone went straight to my heart. It seemed to me a man might suffer much to be loved with such love as this.

In the early afternoon Graeme came to her. She met him with both hands outstretched, saying in a low voice—

"I am very happy."

"Are you sure?" he asked.

"Oh, yes," she said, but her voice was like a sob. "Quite sure."

They talked long together till I saw that Craig must soon be coming, and I called Graeme away. He held her hands, looking steadily into her eyes, and said—

"You are more selfless even than I thought. I will be a better man, someday."

"Yes! You will be a good man. And God will give you work to do."

He bent his head over her hands and stepped back from her as from royalty. He spoke no word for sometime. Then he said with humility that seemed strange in him, "Connor, it is great to conquer oneself. It is a worthwhile goal in life. I am going to try it."

I went back to Craig's with him. Nelson was busy with tea. Craig was writing near the window. He looked up as we came in and nodded an easy good-evening. But Graeme strode to him, put one hand on his shoulder, and held out the other for Craig to take.

After a moment's surprise, Craig rose to his feet, faced him squarely, and took the offered hand in both of his and held it fast without a word. Graeme was the first to speak, and his voice was deep with emotion—

"You are a great man. I'd give something to have your spirit."

Poor Craig stood looking at him, not daring to speak for some moments, then he said quietly—

"Not great, not even good, but thank God, not quite a traitor."

Ten minutes later Craig and I approached Mrs. Mavor's door. She did not hear us coming, but stood near the window gazing up at the mountains. She was dressed in some rich soft stuff, and wore a bunch of wildflowers at her breast. I had never seen her so beautiful. I did not wonder that Craig paused with his foot upon the threshold to look at her.

She turned and saw us. With a glad cry, "Oh, my darling, you have come to me," she came with outstretched arms. I turned away and left quickly, but the cry and the vision were long with me.

Craig went into her house. They were together most of the evening. When he emerged and returned to his cabin, he looked as weary as he had the day before. Their love had, in such a short time, proved a very costly one. Together that night, in agonizing prayer together, it was decided that Mrs. Mavor should go the next week to fulfill her family responsibilities. A miner and his wife were going East and would take her. As my time was long past, I too would join the party.

The camp went into mourning at the news, but it was understood that any display of grief before Mrs. Mavor would be bad form.

When it was suggested by those closest to her that she should perhaps leave quietly and avoid the pain of saying good-bye, she flatly refused.

"I must say good-bye to every man," she insisted. "They

176

love me, and I love them. I have to tell them why it is I must go. They understand duty to family. They must not think I am forsaking them...or him."

It was decided, too, at first, that there should be nothing in the way of a testimonial, but when Craig found out that the men were coming to her with all sorts of extraordinary little presents, he agreed that it would be better that they should unite in one gift. The moment the word spread, contributions began coming in immediately for a ring. Were it not that each man was strictly limited to one dollar, the purse Slavin handed her when Shaw read the address at the farewell supper would have been many times filled with the gold that was pressed upon the committee. There were no speeches at the supper, except one by myself in reply on Mrs. Mavor's behalf. She had given me the words to say, and I was thoroughly prepared, otherwise I would never have got through it. I began in the usual way: "Mr. Chairman, ladies and gentlemen, Mrs. Mavor is—"but I got no further, for at the mention of her name the men stood on the chairs and yelled until they could yell no more. There were over two-hundred-fifty of them, and the effect was overpowering. But I got through my speech.

I remember it well. It began—

"Mrs. Mavor is greatly touched by this mark of your love, and she will wear your ring always with pride." And it ended with—

"She has one request to make, that you will be true to the League, and that you stand close about the man who did most to make it. She wishes me to say that however far away she may have to go, she is leaving her heart in Black Rock, and she can think of no greater joy than to come back to you again."

Then Mrs. Mavor stood and sang *The Sweet By and By.* The men were absolutely still, unwilling to lose so much as a note of the glorious voice they loved to hear. Before the last verse, she said—

"Please sing the refrain with me. I want to carry the memory of your beautiful voices singing these consoling words with me in my heart."

At once the men sat up and cleared their throats. The singing was not good, but at the first sound of the hoarse notes of the men, Craig's head went down over the organ. He was thinking, I suppose, of the days before them when they would long in vain for that thrilling voice that soared high over their own raspy tones. After the voices died away he kept on playing till, half turned toward him, she sang alone once more the refrain in a voice low and sweet and tender, as if for him alone. And so he took it, for he smiled up at her, his old smile full of courage and full of love.

Then for one whole hour she stood saying good-bye to those rough, gentle-hearted men whose inspiration and goodness she had been for five years. It was very wonderful and very quiet. There was no nonsense. In fact, Abe had been heard to declare that he would "throw out any cotton-backed fool who couldn't hold himself down," and further, he had enjoined them all to remember that "her arm wasn't a pump handle."

At last they were all gone, all but her guard of honor—Shaw, Vernon Winton, Geordie, Nixon, Abe, Nelson, Craig, Graeme and myself.

This was the real farewell. For though in the early light of the next morning two hundred men stood silent about the stage, and then as it moved out waved their hats and yelled madly, this was the last touch they had of her hand.

Her place was up on the driver's seat between Abe and Craig, who held little Marjorie on his knee. The rest of the guard of honor were to follow with Graeme's team. It was Winton's fine sense that kept Graeme from following too close. "Let her go out alone," he said, and so we held back and watched her go.

She stood with her back toward Abe's plunging four-horse team, and steadying herself with one hand on Abe's shoulder, gazed down upon the men of Black Rock and from the lumber camp. Her head was bare, her lips parted in a smile, her eyes glowing with their own deep light. And so, as she faced them, erect and smiling, the stage drove away, and Abe swung his team into the canyon road and they saw her no more. A sigh shuddered through the crowd as she moved out of sight.

I close my eyes and see it all again. By some quirk of imagination vision, although I was inside the stage, I felt as though I was one of the crowd, watching as she drove away. It comes back to me like yesterday. The waving crowd of dark-faced men, the plunging horses, and high up beside the driver, the swaying, smiling, waving figure—and about all the mountains, framing the picture with their dark sides and white peaks tipped with the gold of the rising sun. It is a picture I love to recall, but it always calls up another that I can never see but through tears.

It was several days later when the miner and his wife, along with Mrs. Mavor and I and several others, stood waving our last good-byes at the river Landing to those few faithful ones who had accompanied us that far. Among them were my old friend Graeme and my new friends Craig and Nelson and the others.

In my mind's eye I look across that strip of ever-widening water at the small group of men on the wharf, standing with heads uncovered, every man a hero, though not a man of them suspected it—least of all the man who stood in front, strong, resolute, self-conquered. And, gazing long, I think I see him turn again to his place among the men of the mountains, not forgetting, but everyday remembering that love is not all. It is then the tears come.

But because of that picture, two of us at least are better men today.

20.
HOW NELSON CAME HOME

Through the long summer months, though I was surrounded again by the sights and sounds of civilization in Eastern Canada, the mountains and pines were constantly with me.

Through the winter too, as busy as I was with filling in my Black Rock sketches for the railway people, the memory of that stirring life would come over me, and once more I would find myself among the silent pines and the mighty snow-capped peaks. And before me would appear the red-shirted shantymen or dark-faced miners—great, free, bold fellows, driving me almost mad with the desire to seize and fix on my canvas those swiftly changing groups of picturesque figures. But always something in the intense reality of the memory eluded my fingers.

At such times I would drop my sketch, and with an eager brush try to capture a group, a face, a figure. And thus my studio gradually came to be filled with all the men of Black Rock. There they all are about me. Graeme and the men from the woods, Sandy, Baptiste, the Campbells, and in many attitudes and groups of old man Nelson. Craig is there

180

too, and his miners—Shaw, Geordie, Nixon, and poor Billy and the keeper of the League saloon.

It seemed as if I still lived among them, and the illusion was greatly helped by the vivid letters Graeme sent me from time to time. Brief notes came now and then from Craig as well, to whom I had sent a faithful account of how I had brought Mrs. Mavor to her ship bound for England and her husband's family, and her hand that bore the miners' ring, smiling with that deep light in her eyes.

Ah! Those eyes have driven me to despair and made me fear that I am no great painter after all, in spite of what some of my friends tell me. I can get the brow and hair, the mouth and pose. But the eyes! The eyes elude me—and the faces of Mrs. Mavor on my wall, which the men who visit praise and rave over, are not such as I could show to any of the men from the mountains.

Graeme's letters tell me chiefly about Craig and his doings, and about old man Nelson. From Craig I hear about Graeme, and how he and Nelson are standing at his back and doing what they can to fill the gap that never can be filled. The three are much together, I can see, and I am glad for them all, but chiefly for Craig, whose face, grief-stricken but resolute and often gentle as a woman's, will not leave me nor let me rest in peace.

In the spring came the news that the Black Rock mine would be shut down for six months. It grieved me to think how such an occurrence might change the complexion of the place whenever I managed to be able to return—about which I dreamed constantly. But with it came the welcome prospect that the three men who most represented that life would soon visit me, actually in my own home. Graeme's letter said that many of the men had found other work for a time; he had hired on as many as he could in his Lumber Camp, and few wanted to leave. He went on to say that in a month or so he and Nelson might be expected to make an appearance, and Craig would likely follow.

On receiving the great news, I at once went to see young Nelson and his sister, for this was Nelson's home ground as well as my own. He had asked me to visit them, which I had already done on several occasions. Together we proceeded to celebrate the joyful prospect with an especially good dinner. I found great delight in picturing the joy and pride of the old man in these his children, whom he had not seen for fifteen or sixteen years. The mother had died some five years before, then the family farm was sold, and the brother and sister came into the city. Any father might be proud of them.

Nelson's son was a well-made young fellow, handsome enough, thoughtful, and solid-looking. The girl reminded me of her father. The same resolution was seen in mouth and jaw, and the same passion slumbered in the dark grey eyes. She was not beautiful, but she carried herself well, and one would always look at her twice. It would be worth something to see the meeting between father and daughter.

But fate, the greatest artist of all, takes little account of the careful drawing and the bright coloring of our fancy pictures, but with rude hand ravages all, and with one swift sweep paints out the bright and paints in the dark. Such came to my canvas one June night—what unbelievers would call the cruel twist of that fate, what believers would prayerfully accept as the loving, yet mysteriously beyond our ken hand of the Almighty. For after long and anxious waiting for some word from the West, my door suddenly opened and in walked my old friend Leslie Graeme.

His movements reminded me of a spectre, grey and voiceless. I knew instantly something was wrong.

My shout of welcome was choked back by the look in his face, and I could only gaze at him and wait for his word. He gripped my hand, tried to speak, but failed to make words come.

"Sit down, old man," I said, pushing him into my chair, "and take your time."

He obeyed, looking up at me with burning, sleepless eyes. My heart was sore for his misery.

Finally I said, "Come, old chap, it can't be that bad. You're here, safe and sound at any rate." I stopped, and again it was silent. But he shuddered and looked around and groaned.

"What is it, man?" I said. "Where is Nelson?"

At last he spoke, and his words told all.

"He is still at the station," he answered slowly, "in his coffin."

"His coffin?" I echoed, my beautiful pictures of happy reunions all vanishing. "How could—"

"It was all on account of my cursed folly," he groaned bitterly.

"What happened?" I implored.

But ignoring my question, he said, "I must see his children. I have hardly slept for four nights. I hardly know what I am doing, but I cannot rest till I see his children. I promised him. Take me to them."

"Tomorrow will do. Go to sleep now. I'll arrange everything for tomorrow," I said.

"No," he said fiercely. "Tonight!"

In half an hour they were listening, pale and grief-stricken, to the story of their father's death.

Poor Graeme was relentless in his self-condemnation as he told how, through his "cursed folly," old Nelson was killed. Rather than coming directly East, they had detoured south to spend some days in San Francisco before heading across the States and north again. But there in an evil hour Graeme met a companion of other and terrible days, and it was not long till the old fever for drink came upon him.

In vain Nelson warned and pleaded with him. But the reaction from the monotony and poverty of camp life to the excitement and luxury of San Francisco with its bright lights and gambling saloons swung Graeme quite off his feet, and all Nelson could do was to follow from place to place and keep watch.

"And there he would sit," said Graeme in a hard, bitter voice, "waiting and watching often till the grey morning light, while my madness held me fast to the poker table.

"One night," and here he paused a moment, put his face in his hands, and shuddered—"One night my partner and I were playing two men who had beat us earlier. I knew they were cheating but could not detect the exact moment. Hand after hand they won, till I was furious at my stupidity in not being able to catch them. Happening to glance at Nelson in the corner, I caught a meaningful look from him, and looking again, he threw me a signal.

"I knew at once what the fraud was, and next round charged the fellow with it. He said he knew nothing. I stood and struck him, like the fool I was, filled with cheap beer. But before I could draw my gun, his partner had me by the arms. What followed I hardly know. While I was struggling to get free, I saw the man reach for his weapon. But as he drew it, Nelson sprang across the table and took him to the floor. Shots rang out, and when the row was over, three men lay on the floor. One was Nelson. He had taken the shot meant for me."

Again the story paused.

"I got him to a private ward at the nearest hospital," he went on slowly, "had the best doctor in the city, and sent for Craig. He came quickly, for he was not far behind us. But by the time Craig arrived I was beginning to give up hope. Oh, but I was thankful to see Craig come in, and the joy in the old man's eyes as he lay there was beautiful to see. For many days we thought he would live—he wanted so badly to get home. There was no pain and no fear. He would not allow me to reproach myself over what had happened, saying over and over, 'You would have done the same for me'—as I would have, certainly enough—'and it is better me than you. I am old and my life is behind me. You will do much good yet for the boys.' And he kept looking at me till I could only promise to do my best.

I am glad I told him how much good he had done me during the last year. And when Craig told him how he had helped the boys in the camp, and how Sandy and Baptiste and the Campbells would always be better men for his life among them, the old man's face actually shone, as if light were coming through. And with surprise and joy he kept on saying, 'Do you think so? Do you really think so?' Then at the last he talked of Christmas Eve night at the camp. You were there, you remember. Craig had been holding a service, and something happened, I don't know what, but they both knew."

"I know," I said, as I saw again the picture of the old man under the pines, upon his knees in the snow with his face turned up to the stars.

"Whatever it was, it was in his mind at the very last, and I can never forget his face as he turned to Craig. One hears of such things. But I had never put much stock in them myself. But joy and triumph, those are what were in his face as he said, his breath coming short now, 'You said once—He wouldn't fail me—you were right—not once—not once—He stuck to me—I'm glad—thank God—for you—you showed—me—I'll see Him—and—tell Him...'"

"Craig knelt down beside him and smiled warmly through his streaming tears into the dim eyes till they could see no more. He helped the old man through, and he helped me too, that night, thank God!"

And all at once Graeme's voice, hard till that moment, broke down in a sob.

He had all but forgotten us as we listened. He was back beside his dying friend, and all his self-control could not keep back the flowing tears.

"He gave his life for mine," he said.

The brother and sister were quietly weeping, but spoke no word.

I took up the conversation, and told them of what I had known of their father, and how I had seen Nelson's influence throughout Black Rock. They listened eagerly, but still without speaking.

At length Graeme rose to go. Suddenly the girl turned to him, and, impulsively putting out her hand, said—

"Thank you for telling us, but...you must not blame yourself."

"How can you ever forgive me?" gasped Graeme. I brought him to his death!"

"No, no! You must not say so," she replied hurriedly. "You—all of you who knew him well—you helped bring him to life, not death."

"But—" objected Graeme, but she stopped him.

"His was a hard life. He had cut off everything from his past, even us. But these last months—the change—you should have seen his letters—"

Now it was the girl's turn to break down weeping.

"You'll never know," she struggled to go on through her tears, "how much he loved you all—and how much he changed toward us—how he opened his heart again. We *will* see him again, and it will be a glorious reunion. And we have you—all his friends in Black Rock—to thank for giving him something he had so little of all his life—for giving him love."

By this time the tears were burning in Graeme's eyes.

When the time came we carried old man Nelson to his old home in the country, that he might lie by the side of the wife he had loved and wronged. A few friends of his family met us at the wayside station, and followed in sad procession along the country road that wound past farms and through woods, and at last up to the ascent where the quaint old wooden church, black with the rains and snows of many years, stood among its silent markers. The little graveyard sloped gently toward the setting sun, and from it one could see, far on every side, the fields of grain and meadowland that wandered off over softly undulating hills to meet the maple woods at the horizon, dark, green, and cool. Here and there white farmhouses, with great barns standing near, looked out from clustering orchards.

Up the grass-grown walk and through the crowding mounds, over which waved long tangling grass, we bore our friend, then let him gently down into the kindly bosom of mother earth, dark, moist, and warm. The sound of a distant cowbell mingled with the voice of the last prayer. The clods dropped heavily with heart-startling echo. The mound was heaped and shaped by the kindly friends, sharing the task with one another. The long rough sods were laid over and patted into place. The old minister took his farewell in a few words of gentle sympathy. The brother and sister, with lingering looks at the two graves side by side, the old and the new, stepped into the farmer's carriage and drove away. The sexton locked the gate and went home. And finally only the two of us were left outside alone.

We stood looking by Nelson's grave.

After a long silence Graeme spoke.

"Connor," he said, "he did not grudge his life to me —and I think"—and here the words came slowly—"I think I finally am beginning to understand what that statement means *Who loved me and gave Himself for me.*"

Then he took off his hat and said reverently, "By God's help, Nelson's life shall not end, but shall go on. Yes, old man!" he added, looking at the grave, "I'm with you!" And lifting his face up to the calm sky, he said—though now he was speaking neither to Nelson nor to me—"God help me to be true!"

Then he turned and walked briskly away, as one who had pressing business to attend to.

21.
GRAEME'S RETURN HOME

There was more left in that grave than old man Nelson's body.

It seemed to me that Graeme left part, at least, of his old self there, with his dead friend and comrade, in the quiet country churchyard. I waited a long time for the old careless, reckless spirit to reappear, but he was never the same again.

The change was unmistakable, but hard to define. He seemed to have resolved his life into a definite purpose. He was by no means comfortable to be with. He made me feel even more lazy and useless. But I respected him more, and liked him none the less. As a lion he was not a success. He would not roar. This was a trifle disappointing, both to me and to his friends, who had been awaiting his visit with eager expectation of tales of thrilling and bloodthirsty adventure. He had not been back in his home city for many years, but his numerous friends were true as ever.

His first days were spent in making right, or as nearly right as he could, the break that drove him to the West. The old firm for which he had once worked behaved really well.

Graeme never confided all the details of the problem to me, but his former employers proved the restoration of their confidence in his integrity and ability by offering him a place in the firm, which, however, he would not accept. Then, when he felt clean, as he said, he headed back for his old home, taking me with him.

During the railway journey of four hours he hardly spoke. When we had left the town of our destination behind, and were installed in our carriage and fairly well along the country road that led toward the village of his home ten miles away, where he had spent the years of his childhood and youth, then his speech began to come in a great glow.

All at once he was like a lad returning from his first term at college. His very face wore the boy's open, innocent, earnest look that used to attract men to him during his University days. His delight in the fields and woods, in the sweet country air and the sunlight, was without bound. How often we had driven this road together in the old days!

Every turn of the lane was familiar. The swamp where the tamaracks stood straight and slim out of their beds of moss; the brule, as we used to call it, where the pine-stumps, huge and blackened, were half-hidden by the new growth of poplars and soft maples; the big hill, where we used to get out and walk when the roads were bad; the orchards, where the harvest apples were best and most accessible—all had their memories.

It was one of those perfect afternoons that so often come in the early Canadian summer, before Nature grows weary with the heat. The white gravel road was trimmed on both sides with turf of living green grass, closely cut by the sheep that wandered in flocks along its whole length. Beyond the picturesque snake-fences stretched the fields of springing grain, of varying shades of green, with here and there a dark brown patch, marking a turnip field or summer fallow. Farther back were the woods of maple and beech and elm, with occasionally the tufted top of a mighty pine, the lonely representative of a vanished race, standing clear above the humbler trees.

As we came nearer home, the houses became familiar. Everyone had its tale: we had eaten or slept in most of them. We had sampled apples and cherries and plums from their orchards, openly as guests, or secretly as young marauders, under cover of the night—the more delightful way, I fear.

Ah, happy days! Those innocent crimes and fleeting remorses, how bravely we faced them, and how gaily we lived them, and how yearningly we looked back at them now!

The sun was just dipping into the tree-tops of the distant woods behind us as we came to the top of the last hill that overlooked the valley in which lay the village of Riverdale. Wooded hills stood about it on three sides, and, where the hills faded out, there lay the mill pond sleeping and smiling in the sun. Through the village ran the white road, up past the old frame church, and on to the white manse standing among the trees.

That was Graeme's home, and mine too, for I had never known another worthy of the name. We held up our team to look down over the valley, with its rampart of wooded hills, its shining pond, and its nestling village, and on past to the church and the manse, hiding among the trees. The beauty, the peace, the warm, loving homeliness of the scene came about our hearts, but, being men, we could find no words.

"Let's go!" cried Graeme, and down the hill we tore and rocked and swayed to the surprise of the steady team, whose education from the earliest years had impressed upon their minds the criminality of attempting to do anything but walk carefully down a hill, at least for two-thirds of the way. Through the village in a cloud of dust we swept, catching a glimpse of a familiar face here and there, and flinging a greeting as we passed, leaving the owner of the face rooted to his place in astonishment at the sight of Graeme whirling on in his old-time reckless manner. Only old Duncan MacLeod was equal to the moment, for as Graeme called out, "Hello, Dunc!" the old man lifted up his hands and called back in an awed voice, "Bless my soul! Is it yersel'?"

"Stands his whisky well, poor old chap!" was Graeme's comment.

As we neared the church and cemetery he pulled up his team, and we went quietly past the sleepers there, then again on the full run down the gentle slope, over the little brook, and up to the gate. He had hardly got his team pulled up before, flinging me the lines, he was out over the side, for coming down the walk, with her hands lifted high, was a dainty little lady with the face of an angel.

In a moment Graeme had her in his arms. I heard the faint cry, "My boy! My boy!" and got down on the other side to attend to the horse, surprised to find my hands trembling and my eyes full of tears. Back upon the steps stood an old gentleman with white hair and flowing beard, handsome, straight, and stately—Graeme's father, waiting his turn.

"Welcome home, my lad," was his greeting, as he kissed his son on the cheek, and the tremor of his voice, and the sight of the two men embracing, like women, sent me to my horses' heads.

"There's Connor, mother!" shouted out Graeme, and the dainty little lady, in her black silk and white lace, came towards me quickly with outstretched hands.

"You too are welcome home," she said, and kissed me.

I stood with my hat off, saying something about being glad to come, but wishing I could get away before I should make quite a fool of myself. For as I looked down upon the beautiful face, pale except for a faint flush upon each faded cheek, and read the story of pain endured and conquered, and as I thought of all the long years of waiting and of vain hoping, I found my throat dry and sore, and the words would not come. But her quick sense needed no words, and she came to my help. I wondered if Sandy's story about the Prodigal that night in the stable had come back into Graeme's mind as it suddenly had to mine.

"You will find Jack at the stable," said Graeme's mother smiling. "He ought to have been here."

The stable! Why had I not thought of that before? Thankfully now my words came—

"Yes, certainly, I'll find him, Mrs. Graeme, I suppose he's as much of a scapegrace as ever," and off I went to look up Graeme's younger brother, who had given every promise in the old days of developing into as stirring a rascal as one could desire. But as I found out later, he had not lived all these years in his mother's home for nothing.

"Oh, Jack's a good boy," she answered, smiling again as she turned toward the other two, now waiting for her upon the walk.

22.
GRAEME'S NEW BIRTH

The week that followed was a happy one for us all.

For the mother it was full to the brim with joy. Her sweet face was full of contentment, and in her eyes rested a great peace. Our days were spent driving about among the hills, or strolling through the maple woods, or down into the tamarack swamp where the pitcher plants and the swamp lilies and the marigolds waved above the deep moss.

In the evenings we sat under the trees on the lawn till the stars came out and the night dews drove us in. Like two lovers, Graeme and his mother would wander off together, leaving Jack and me to each other. Jack was studying for the ministry, desiring to follow in his father's footsteps, and was really a fine, manly fellow, with his brother's turn for rugby. I took to him immediately. After the day was over we would gather about the supper table and the talk would be of all things under heaven—art, football, theology. The mother would often strike out the lead in the conversation. How quick she was, how bright her fancy, how subtle her intellect, and through it all a gentle grace, very winning and beautiful to see.

Do what I would, however, I could not get Graeme to talk about the mountains and his life there.

"My lion will not roar, Mrs. Graeme," I complained.

"You should twist his tail," said Jack.

"That is the difficulty, Jack," said his mother, "to get hold of his tale."

"Where does such a comic outlook come from, mother," laughed Jack. "Is it this baleful Western influence?"

"I shall reform," she said brightly.

"But seriously, Graeme," I remonstrated, "you ought to tell your family of your life there—that free, glorious life in the mountains."

"Free! Glorious!" he exclaimed. "To some men, perhaps." Then he fell back into silence.

But I saw the new Graeme emerge the night he talked theology with his father. The old minister was a splendid Calvinist, of heroic type, and as he went on about God's sovereignty and the chosen elect, his face glowed and his voice rang out.

Graeme listened intently, now and then putting in a question, as one would a keen knife-thrust into a foe. But the old man knew his ground, and moved easily among his ideas, demolishing with jaunty grace the enemy as he appeared. In the full flow of his triumphant argument, Graeme turned to him with sudden seriousness.

"Look here, father. I was born a Calvinist, and I can't see how anyone with a level head can believe anything but that God has some idea as to how He wants to run His universe, and He means to carry out His idea. But what would you do in a case like this?" Then he told him the story of poor Billy Breen, his fight and his defeat.

"Would you preach about the doctrine of the elect to that chap?" he concluded.

The mother's eyes were shining with tears.

The old gentleman blew his nose like a trumpet, and then said gravely—

"No, my boy, you don't feed babes with meat. But what came to him?"

Graeme asked me to go on with the tale. After I had finished the story of Billy's final triumph and of Craig's part in it, they sat long and silent, till the minister, clearing his throat hard and blowing his nose more like a trumpet than ever, said with great emphasis—

"Thank God for such a man in such a place! I wish there were more like him."

"I would like to get you out there, father," said Graeme. "You'd make them listen! But I doubt you'd have much time to preach about the election."

"Yes, yes! I would love to have a chance to preach to those poor lads. If only I were twenty years younger!"

"It is worth a man's life," said Graeme earnestly. "Why don't you come with me? You too, Jack."

"With you?" questioned his mother. It was the first hint he had given of his purpose. "You are going back?"

"What! As a missionary?" said Jack.

"Not to preach," said Graeme. "I'm not orthodox enough. Besides, I still have my lumber camp. But perhaps I can occasionally lend a hand to some poor chap, and help a few of them to see above the mountains."

"Could you not find work nearer home, my boy?" asked the father. "There is plenty of both kinds near us here."

"Lots of work, but not mine, I fear," answered Graeme, keeping his eyes away from his mother's face. "A man must do the work God gives him."

His voice was quiet and resolute, and glancing at the beautiful face at the end of the table, I saw in the pale lips and yearning eyes that the mother was offering up her first-born in that ancient manner of sacrifice. But not all the agony of the sacrifice would wring from her an entreaty or complaint in the hearing of her sons. That was for other ears and for the silent hours of the night. And the next morning when she came down to meet us her face was wan and weary, but it wore the peace of victory and a glory not of earth. Her greeting was full of dignity, sweet and gentle. When she came to my friend, she lingered over him and kissed him twice. That was all that any of us ever saw of that sore fight.

At the end of the week I took my leave of them. The responsibilities of my assignment with the railroad were calling me, but I knew I would be back and thus the farewells were not painful. When Graeme waved to me as I turned back for the last time, his face wore such a look of innocent joy. I marveled that he had ever left this place in pain. Surely these would be healing months for him! His two wonderful parents had, like the father of the Prodigal, opened their arms and hearts wide to him—as had his brother Jack—and I could see the change almost visibly as he drank in the love he had previously been unable to fathom.

When I returned at the end of the summer, to see Graeme before he left again for the West, the farewells were considerably more tear-filled and poignant.

After we finished breakfast on our final morning, Mr. Graeme prayed according to his invariable custom. He understood that a man must give up pretenses when he undertakes to address the Almighty; there is no place in prayer for pretended cheerfulness and courage. As the old man prayed, barriers were broken down by the rush of emotions that had till then been held in check by force of will. The brave little mother broke down into quiet weeping, while the father commended us as we departed "from his home this day to the care and keeping of the Great Father from whom distance cannot separate and to whom no land is strange."

I could see Graeme was losing grip of himself too, but then the prayer rose into a great strain of thanksgiving for "the love that reached down from Heaven to save a world of lost men, and for the noble company who are giving their lives to bring this love near to men's hearts." Then we all grew quiet, and under the steadying of that prayer the farewells were easier.

"Good-bye, Leslie, my son. God be with you and keep you and make you a blessing to many," said the old gentleman. His voice was steady, but he immediately turned aside and blew his nose like a trumpet, remarking on the chilly morning air. The mother's farewell was without a word. She reached up and put her arms about her son's neck, kissed him, and then let him go.

I said good-bye to the dear lady last of all.

She hesitated just a moment, then suddenly put her hands upon my shoulders and kissed me too, saying softly, "You are his friend; you will come visit me sometimes?"

"Gladly, if I may," I hastened to answer, for the sweet brave face was too much to bear, and till she left us for that world of which she was a part, I kept my word.

We were nearly halfway to the city when suddenly Graeme burst out—

"Connor, do you know, I have just these past two months discovered my mother! I don't think I have ever known her till this summer."

"All the more blind you have been," I answered.

"Yes, that is true," he said slowly, "but you cannot see until you have eyes."

Before he set out again for the West and we two parted ways, I gave him a supper party in the city, inviting all our old friends who had been with us in the University days. I knew Graeme had changed, but I was hardly prepared for what was to transpire before the night was through.

The supper was of the best, the wines I had chosen first class. But as the evening wore on I began to wish I had left out the wines, for the men began to drop an occasional oath, though I had let them all know that Graeme was not the man he had once been.

Things went on, however, and Graeme talked and paid little attention, until one of our friends by the name of Rattray—whom we always called "Rat" for short—swore by that name most sacred of all ever borne by man. Then Graeme opened upon him in a cool, slow way—

"What an awful fool a man is, to damn things as you do, Rat. Things are not damned. It is men who are, and that is too horrible to be talked about. But when a man flings out of his foul mouth the name of Jesus Christ"—and here he lowered his voice—"it's a shame. It's even more than a shame, it's a crime."

There was dead silence. Then Rattray attempted a startled reply—

"I—I suppose you may be right, it is bad form. But crime is rather strong, it seems to me."

"Not if you consider who it is," said Graeme without flinching.

"Oh, come now," broke in one of the other men who had had more than his share of the wine, "religion is a good enough thing, and I believe necessary for the race. But no one takes seriously those old myths any longer."

"I fooled with notions like that for some time," said Graeme. "But it won't do. You can't build a religion that will take the devil out of a man on a myth. I don't want to argue about it, but I am quite convinced of the reality. Besides, I'm not talking about religion. My father was a clergyman, as you all know. And I came up in the church as a lad. I know all about *religion*. No, I'm talking about something quite different from all that. No, your myth theory is not reasonable, and besides, it won't work."

"Will the other work?" asked Rattray.

"I've seen it," said Graeme. "I've seen men's lives changed."

"Where?" challenged Rattray. "I've never seen such a thing."

"I'll tell you boys," said Graeme. "I want you to know why I believe what I do."

Then he told them the story of old man Nelson, from the old coast days, before I knew him, to the end, and how

198

different he had been from the moment he had prayed in the snow on Christmas Eve. He told the story well. The stern fight and victory of the life, the self-sacrifice and pathos of the death appealed to some of these men.

"That's why I believe in Jesus Christ. That's why I know *He* is no myth, because He is changing lives still— Nelson's and mine. And that's why I think it is a crime to fling his name about."

"Look here, old chap," said Rattray, "for all I know you may be right. I've known a few religious men in my time, but most of those who go in for that sort of thing are not of much account."

"For ten years, Rat," said Graeme in a downright matter-of-fact way, "you and I and men like us have tried this sort of thing"—tapping a bottle—"and we got out of it all there is to be got, paid well for it too. You know it's not good enough, and the more you go in for the drinking life, the more you curse yourself. One of the best men I ever knew is dead now because I was such a fool and filled myself up on cheap whisky. So I am finally awake, reborn as the Book says, and I have quit this and am giving my life to serve another Master."

"What! Going in for preaching?"

"Not much. I'll do whatever comes to me, and lend what hand I can to fellows on the rocks that haven't seen the truth yet."

"But, I say, Graeme," persisted our friend we all called Beetles, "you don't really mean to say you go in for the whole thing—Jonah, you know, the sun stopping in the sky, walking on water, and the rest of it?"

Graeme hesitated, then said—

"I haven't much of a creed, Beetles. I don't really know exactly what I believe about one doctrine or another. But I do know that good is good and bad is bad, and that good and bad are not the same. And I know that a man is a fool to follow the one, and a wise man to follow the other. And I know that Jesus Christ is good, and I've seen enough of the devil's work to know that he is bad. And I believe God is at the back of any man who wants to get done with the bad from his life. And I believe Jesus Christ is at the side of any such man, helping him with every step. So that's where I am, and He's got my hand and I'm holding on tight. And my new Chief is out there now, as He is everywhere, over His ears in His work among men, and He must have help at once."

When I told Craig about this night many months later, when he was on his way back from his Old Land trip to join Graeme in the mountains, and about Graeme's unembarrassed declaration of faith before all his old friends, he threw up his head in the old way and said, "It was well done. It must have been worth seeing. Old man Nelson's work is far from done yet."

Then he made me go over the whole scene again.

But when I told Mrs. Mavor, the next time I saw her, she could only say, "Old things are passed away, all things are become new." And the light glowed in her eyes till I could not be sure of their color.

23.
TRAVELS

A man with a conscience is often provoking, sometimes impossible. Persuasion is lost upon him. He will not get angry, and he looks at one with such a faraway expression in his face that in striving to persuade him one feels earthly, even fiendish.

At least this was my experience with Craig. He spent a week with me just before sailing for England, for the purpose, as he said, of getting some of the coal dust and other grime out of him. I knew, however, that Graeme's decision played heavily in his plans. He wanted Leslie to have the opportunity to grow in his resolve as a fledgling gospel missionary to his fellows by standing on his own feet a while.

Craig made me angry the last night of his stay, and all the more that he remained quite sweetly unmoved. We talked of the old days, of what he hoped to do when he returned to the mountains. We talked of Nelson and of course about Graeme and his commitment to "the cause of Christ," as Craig called it. We talked of everything, in fact, but the one thing, about the only thing, to my mind, that really mattered. About that we said not a word till, bending low to poke my fire and hide my face, I finally plunged in—

"You will see her, of course?"

He made no pretense of not understanding, but answered—

"Of course. She is near London and I plan to visit her."

"There's really no sense in her staying over there," I suggested.

"She is a wise woman," he said, as if carefully considering the question.

"Many landlords never see their tenants, and they are none the worse."

"The landlords?"

"No, the tenants."

"Probably, having such landlords."

"As for the old lady," I continued, "there must be someone around to whom it would be a Godsend to care for her."

"Now, Connor," he said quietly, "don't go on. We have gone over all there is to be said. Nothing new has happened. Don't turn it all up again. The path lies straight before my feet. Should I leave the way marked out for me? I would only disappoint you—and all of them—if I did."

I knew he was thinking of Graeme and the lads in the mountains he had taught to be true men. It did not help my frustration, but it checked my speech.

After all, you know," he went on, "there are great compensations for the losses one encounters for the sake of the Kingdom of Heaven. Jesus said so many times. But for the loss of a good conscience toward God—what can ever make up for that?"

All the same, I could not help but hope for some better result from his visit to Britain. The months passed, however, and when I looked into Craig's face again I knew that nothing had changed, and that he had come back to take up his life in the West—alone, and more resolutely hopeful than ever.

But the time away from the mines and the mountains had left its mark upon him too. He was a broader and deeper man. He had been living and thinking with men of larger ideas and richer culture, and he was far too quick in sympathy with life to remain untouched by his surroundings. He was more tolerant of opinions others than his own, but more unrelenting in his faithfulness to conscience, in his determination to obey God with his whole being, and more impatient of half-heartedness and self-indulgence. He was full of reverence for the great scholars and great leaders of men he had come to know. I could tell after just a short time with him that when he returned to the mountains, which he was determined to do, it would be to take, not only the gospel to the hard-working men there, but a little more of culture as well. The sabbatical had clearly strengthened him for the work God had given him.

"Great, noble fellows they are, and extraordinarily modest," he said. "That is, the really great are modest. There are plenty of the other sort, neither great nor modest. And the books to be read, Connor! I am quite hopeless about my reading. It gave me a queer sensation to shake hands with a man who had written a great book; to hear him make commonplace remarks, to witness a faltering in knowledge—one expects these men to know everything—and to experience respectful kindness at his hands!"

After a while we paused and looked at each other.

"Well?" I said.

He understood me.

"Yes," he answered slowly. "Doing great work. Everyone worships her just as we do, and she is making them all do something worthwhile, as she used to make us."

He spoke cheerfully and readily as if he were repeating a well-learned lesson, but he could not humbug me. I felt the heartache in the cheerful tone.

"Tell me about her," I said, for I knew that if he would talk it would do him good.

And talk he did, often forgetting me, till, as I listened, I found myself looking again into the fathomless eyes, and hearing again the heart-searching voice. I saw her go in and out of the little red-tiled cottages and down the narrow back lanes of the village outside London. I heard her voice in a sweet, low song by the bed of a dying child, or pouring forth floods of music in the great new hall of the factory town near by. But I could not see, though he tried to show me, the stately gracious lady receiving the country folk in her home. He did not linger over that scene, but went back again to the gate-cottage where she had taken him one day to see Billy Breen's mother.

"I found the old woman knew all about me," he said, "but there were many things about Billy she had never heard, and I was glad to put her right on some points."

He sat silent for a little, looking into the coals, then went on in a soft, quiet voice—"It brought back the mountains and the old days to hear Billy's tones in his mother's voice."

"And then," he went on, "to see—her—sitting there in the very dress she wore the night of the League, you remember—some soft stuff with black lace about it—and to hear her sing as she did for Billy!"

His voice broke unexpectedly, but in a moment he was master of himself and begged me to forgive his break.

"I am getting selfish and weak," he said. "I must get to work. There is much to do. I must just keep myself from getting useless and lazy."

"Useless and lazy!" I said to myself, thinking of my life beside his. And for many days after Craig had left again for Black Rock those words of his goaded me into more regular work than I had done for a long time.

So I again found myself alone, but with my heart torn in two directions, toward the East and toward the West.

Graeme's letters were as inspiring as Craig's. Many of the old gang were still with them, though new men came in all the time, ever renewing the challenge. A new saloon keeper had come to try to resurrect Slavin's old business. Thus the business of the League was as needed as ever. Craig told me what great work Graeme had carried on in his absence. Graeme said what a profound pleasure it was to have Craig back again. From each I gleaned a picture of both men laboring in the harvest fields together, winning the hearts of men, watching by them when sick, making their lives strong, helping them to fight against the alcohol which seemed an ever present temptation, and giving them the courage to die well when their hour came.

One day these letters proved too much for me, and I packed away my paints and brushes, and vowed to the Lord that I would be "useless and lazy" no longer, but would do something with myself. Whether to go East or West I hardly knew. But upon reflection, I realized that I *would* walk the streets of Black Rock again someday. On the other hand, I might never again have the opportunity to see London or Paris or Vienna.

Whether those were the only motivating factors, or whether there was one whom I felt compelled to see, I leave my reader to decide. But the consequence was that I chose the eastern direction, and thus found myself within four weeks on the streets of London, asking myself more diligently than I ever had just what I intended to make of my life. I had finished being a fool, I hoped, at least a fool of the useless kind. The letter that came from Graeme, in reply to my request for a position with him, was characteristic of the man, both new and old, full of gay humor and of the most earnest welcome to the work. It found me still in London.

"Though I must warn you," he concluded, "that there is far more to be done these days than felling trees and making lumber. That is a mere sideline now. The real work is for the hearts and souls of men. It is *that* work in which it is my prayer you will join me."

Mrs. Mavor's reply was like herself—

"I knew you would not long be content with the making of pictures. I knew the day would come when you would join your friends in the West, helping to build lives that the world needs so sorely."

Her last words touched me strangely—

"Be sure you are always thankful for your privilege. It will be good to think of you all, with the glorious mountains about you, and Christ's own work in your hands. Ah, how we would like to be able to choose our work, and the place in which to do it!"

The longing in her soul did not appear in the words, but I could tell how deep and how constant it was. I knew I had grown by the fact that in reply I gave her no bidding to rejoin our band, but rather praised the work she was doing in her place.

For the remainder of the summer I traveled about on the Continent, with the result that I fell out of contact with all my correspondents. When I arrived back in London, I found two letters awaiting me, both of which made my heart beat quick, but with such different feelings. The first was from Graeme, telling me that Craig had been very ill. Mrs. Mavor's letter told me of the death of the old lady who had been her care for the past two years, and of her intention, now that she was able, to spend some months in her old home in Edinburgh.

I made arrangements the next morning to take the train north to Scotland immediately.

24.
HOMECOMING

Before I had time to think about the wisdom or implications of my actions, I was in Edinburgh.

I took a cheap room the moment I arrived, then sought her. But she was not home—I was told she was giving a "performance" that night.

I asked directions, and thus soon found myself in a miserable, dingy, dirty little hall running off an alley in the historic Cowgate, redolent of the glories of the city's splendid past, and of the various odors of the evil-smelling present. I was there to hear Mrs. Mavor sing to the crowd of street urchins that thronged the streets and alleys in the neighborhood and that had been gathered into a sort of club by "a fine leddie frae the West End," for the love of Christ.

I can recall nothing of the program of the evening. But the memory gallery of my mind contains a vivid picture of that face—sad, beautiful, alight with the deep glow of her eyes, as she stood and sang to that lost, pitiful crowd. As I sat upon the window-ledge listening to the voice with its flowing melody, my thoughts were far away, and I was looking down once more upon the eager, coal-grimed faces in the rustic little church in Black Rock. I choked on the emotions that welled up, and found myself swallowing hard. I was brought back to myself by an audible whisper from a little girl nearby to her mother—

"Mither! See yon man. He's cryin'."

When I awoke from my daze, she was singing—

"There's nae sorrow there, Jean,
There's neither cauld nor care, Jean,
The day is aye fair in
The Land o' the Leal." [true, loyal]

A land of fair, warm days, untouched by sorrow and care, would be heaven indeed to these poverty-stricken dwellers of the Cowgate. I could see by their faces that she had given them hope, and perhaps many of them new life, just as she had the men of Black Rock.

The rest of that evening is hazy to me, till I found myself opposite Mrs. Mavor at her fire, reading Graeme's letter to her. Then all becomes suddenly vivid again in my mind.

I could not keep the truth from her. I knew it would be folly to try. So I read straight on till I came to the words:

"He has mountain fever, whatever that may be, and it is doubtful he will put up again. If I can, I shall take him home to my mother, for he needs more nursing than I am able—"

Suddenly she interrupted me, and stretched out her hand, saying, "Oh, please—let me read it!"

I gave her the letter. In another minute she had finished, and began almost breathlessly—

"My life is all changed now. My mother-in-law is gone. She needs me no longer. My lawyer tells me that there were some unfortunate investments, and that there has come up all at once a dire need for a great deal of money, so that the estates or the factory must go. My cousin has everything in the works—his iron works, you know. I would be wrong to have him suffer. I shall give up the estates..."

She paused.

"And come with me?" I cried, hardly believing it possible.

"When do you sail?"

"Next week," I answered eagerly.

She looked at me for a few moments, and into her eyes there came a light soft and tender, as she said—

"I shall go with you."

And so she did. I cabled Graeme immediately, urging him to tell Craig to hang on.

No old Roman in all the glory of a triumph carried a prouder heart than I, as I bore her and her little one, now a beautiful child of four, from the train to Graeme's waiting carriage, crying—

"I've got her!"

But he merely stood waving his hat and shouting—

"He's all right!" at which Mrs. Mavor grew white. But when she and Leslie shook hands, the red was in her cheek again. She had concealed her rising emotion well. But not completely.

"It was the cable that did it," Graeme went on. "Connor always was a great doctor! Good prescription—after mountain fever try a cablegram!"

The red grew yet deeper in the beautiful face beside us.

Never did the country look so lovely. It was even more beautiful than when Graeme and I had driven this way the year before. Yet at this moment I was so full of the person beside me, and fuller still of anticipation for what awaited her, that I must confess the wondrous scenery sped by me. The woods were in their gayest autumn dress, the brown fields were bathed in a purple haze, the air was sweet and fresh with a suspicion of the coming frosts of winter. But in spite of all the road seemed long, and it was as if hours had elapsed before our eyes fell upon the white manse standing among the golden leaves.

"Let the horses go again," I cried as Graeme paused to take in the view, and down the sloping dusty road we flew on the dead run.

"Reminds one of Abe's stage," said Graeme, as we drew up at the gate.

But I found no voice to answer him, for my eyes were now on the beautiful little woman hastening toward us from the gate, and then I was introducing to each other the two best women in the world I had ever known. It seemed they should already have known one another! As indeed, in the spirit, I think they did the moment their eyes met. In another moment the two women had disappeared inside.

As I was about to rush into the house, Graeme seized me by the collar, saying—

"Hold on, Connor! You forget your place. Your turn to see him will come next."

Embarrassed at my impulsiveness, I stopped and asked, "Where is he?"

"At this present moment?" he asked me in a shocked voice. "Why, Connor, you surprise me. You are even thicker than I imagined!"

"Oh, I see!"

"Where else would he be?"

I laughed.

"And," he went on gravely, "you may trust my mother to be discreetly attending to her domestic duties. She is a great woman, my mother."

I had no doubt of it, for at that instant she came out to us, holding little Marjorie by the hand.

"You have shown Mrs. Mavor to her room, mother, I hope," said Graeme. But she only smiled and said—

"Run away with your horses, you silly boy," at which he solemnly shook his head. "Ah, mother, you are a cunning one—who would have thought it of you?"

That evening the manse overflowed with joy, and the days that followed were like dreams set to sweet music.

But for sheer wild delight, nothing in my memory can quite come up to the reception organized by Graeme, with assistance from Nixon, Shaw, Sandy, Abe, Geordie, and Baptiste, in honor of the arrival in camp of Mr. and Mrs. Jim Craig.

In my opinion it added something to the occasion, that after all the cheers for Mr. and Mrs. Craig had died away, and after all the hats had come down, Baptiste, who had never taken his eyes from that radiant face, should suddenly have swept the crowd into a perfect storm of cheers by excitedly seizing his wool cap, and calling out in his shrill voice—

"By gar! Tree cheer for Mrs. Mavor!"

And for many a day the men of Black Rock would easily fall into the old and well-loved name. But up and down the mines of the region, and into the lumber camps of the mountains, and even into far-off towns and villages, the new name became as dear as the old had ever been when it was known only to the men of Black Rock.

Those old days are long since gone into the dim distance of the past. They will not come again, for quieter times have come to me. But often in my pensive moments I feel my heart pause in its beat to hear again that strong, clear voice, like the sound of a trumpet, bidding us to be men. And I think of them all: Graeme—their chief—Sandy, Baptiste, Geordie, Abe, the Campbells, Nixon, Shaw—all stronger and better men for their knowing of him, and especially for their knowing of Him of whose truth and love Craig went to the mountains to tell. Then I think of Billy asleep under the pines, and of old man Nelson with the long grass waving over him in the quiet churchyard.

It is at such times that all my nonsense leaves me, and I bless the Lord for all His benefits, but chiefly for the day I

met the missionary of Black Rock in the lumber camp
among the Selkirk Mountains.

Sunrise Books is committed to offering our readers quality, wholesome books. If you enjoyed this one, we hope you will try another Sunrise title.

Being in the bookstore business ourselves (Sunrise still operates out of the mail room and garage of our retail Christian bookstore), we always stress our hope that you will buy from your own local Christian bookstore. The bookstore ministry is a valuable one to every community and they need your support. However, if you do not have a store easily accessible to you, we at Sunrise are happy to send you our books. Below are listed Sunrise's titles currently available and some that are on the way.

SUNRISE BOOKS, PUBLISHERS CURRENT LIST OF TITLES (1988)

"Ann of the Prairie" Series

Vol. 1	**This Rough New Land**	by Kenneth Sollitt	ISBN 0-940652-03-X
Vol. 2	**Our Changing Lives**	by Kenneth Sollitt	ISBN 0-940652-04-8
Vol. 3	**These Years of Promise**	by Nick Harrison with Kenneth Sollitt	ISBN 0-940652-05-6

"Stories of Yesteryear" Series

Vol. 1	**Jim Craig's Battle for Black Rock**	by Ralph Connor	ISBN 0-940652-06-4
Vol. 2	**Thomas Skyler: Foothills Preacher**	by Ralph Connor	ISBN 0-940652-07-2
Vol. 3	**The Man From Glengarry**	by Ralph Connor	available 1989
Vol. 4	**The Prospector**	by Ralph Connor	available 1989
Vol. 5	**The Doctor**	by Ralph Connor	available 1990
Vol. 6	**Glengarry School Days**	by Ralph Connor	available 1990

The "Sunrise Centenary Editions" of the Works of George MacDonald
Leatherbound collectors editions of the original works of this best-selling 19th century Scottish author, available as a handsome uniform set for the first time this century. Single copy prices of these heirloom editions, $27.50. Member subscriptions rates are available at a reduced rate. Printings are in an individually numbered, limited basis, so write for details and currently available titles in this growing collection.

The Sunrise "Masterline" Series
Studies and essays about George MacDonald, his life, and his works by such leading MacDonald scholars and authorities as Rolland Hein, Michael Phillips, Richard Reis, and MacDonald's own sons. Write for details and a listing of titles in this growing series of important books.